CANADIAN
SOCIAL
STRUCTURE:

A
STATISTICAL
PROFILE

CANADIAN SOCIAL STRUCTURE:
A Statistical Profile

COMPILED AND WITH AN INTRODUCTION
AND COMMENTARY BY
JOHN PORTER

The Carleton Library No. 32 / McClelland and Stewart Limited

CONTENTS

Preface

Preface

Peoples and places have been described in prose, poetry and song. They have been written about by travellers, essayists, journalists, historians and politicians. Societies can also be described by statistics. Statistics are not the easiest way to learn about a country, but they are likely to provide a more accurate picture and are, therefore, of prime importance to the serious student of society. It is this quantitative approach which distinguishes social science from *belles lettres*.

This short book attempts to provide a statistical profile of Canada. It is hoped it may be of use to students and of interest to those who want to learn about the country.

The main part of the book is a collection of statistical tables arranged according to some of the major categories and concepts by which social scientists analyse large-scale social systems. The tables are grouped in ten sections lettered from A to J and are preceded by a brief commentary which tries only to highlight certain features of the data rather than to provide an exhaustive examination of their meaning and implications. There is also a brief discussion of the use, collection and comparability of statistics.

I am very grateful to Ann Kitchen for her examination of statistical sources and for her work on the initial preparation of many of the tables. I am very much indebted to my colleague, Muni Frumhartz, for his advice and comments on the tables and the text. I must also acknowledge small research grants from the Social Science Research Council of Canada and from Carleton University.

JOHN PORTER
Carleton University
February 1967

Introduction: Working with Statistics

Statistical tables are like skeletons. Perhaps that is the reason so many people view them with awe. They are like skeletons because they outline the framework of very complex systems of social life. Like other complex systems, societies are composed of sets of interrelated structures. For societies these structures involve human actions and interactions. Human beings with their needs, satisfactions, frustrations and values are the flesh and blood of the social framework, and it is their social behaviour which is the subject matter of sociology. Consequently, just as our knowledge of bodily structures would be limited if investigation were confined to skeletons, our knowledge of human society would be very inadequate if we did not extend inquiry beyond basic statistical materials.

Tables, such as those collected in this volume, represent an initial ordering of the facts about a large-scale social system; in this sense, they are an arrangement of macro-sociological data. Sociologists, of course, do not confine themselves to the analysis of very large nation-states. They are interested, also, in various smaller groups. Statistics are used in the analysis of these micro-social systems as well (small groups in experimental laboratories, for example), but such analyses are not our concern here.

Since they are an initial ordering of social facts, basic statistical tables can indicate possible avenues of investigation. For example, a table showing the age and sex distribution of the labour force tells us, in a very broad way, how many men and women participate in the productive processes of the society, or at least in that part of the economy in which people work for pay. If the table indicates also that a large number of women in the normal child-bearing and child-rearing years is in the labour force working for pay rather than at home working without pay, we have an indication of the extent to which family life does not fit the stereotyped picture of the mother simply providing services in the home for all other family members. Families with mothers in the labour force may have a different structure from those with mothers at home, and hence become an interesting subject for sociological research.

To take another example, a table showing the occupational and educational composition of the immigrant and emigrant labour force – that is, those of working age who are coming into or moving out of the country – provides the broad picture of the movement of specialized manpower. It could show the degree to which the society is losing people in whose training it has invested through its educational institutions, the so-called "brain drain." On the other hand, it might show a "brain gain" in the form of large numbers of already trained people being brought in from abroad, a condition which may suggest some inadequacy in its educational system.

These two examples illustrate the interrelatedness of broad structures such as the economy, the educational system, the labour force, the family and so forth. Each of these structures makes some essential contribution to the working and continuance of the total social system. That is, each has a set of functions, and an inadequate functioning in any one tends to have repercussions in some other part as it seeks to adjust to a new or unsatisfactory situation. Obviously, if we are going to learn a great deal about the functioning or malfunctioning of these interrelated institutions, we have to go far beyond the statistical tables themselves, but the latter are invaluable in sketching the broad picture of social life.

As well as outlining the basic structures of a society, statistical tables can indicate how these structures change. For example, Table E5 shows the number of people in Canada employed at two points in time in different sectors of the economic system. The table is a simple way of stating the fundamental changes which have taken place in the kinds of work which Canadians do. It shows that between 1946 and 1963 employment in all industries combined increased by 36 per cent, but that this was made up of an 87 per cent increase within the service-producing industries and scarcely any increase at all within the goods-producing industries. Most striking of all, employment in the secondary industries went up by 44 per cent, while in the primary industries it actually went down by 40 per cent. The loss of employment in the primary industries reflected the declining importance, relative to other industries in the

Canadian economy, of logging, fishing, mining and, in particular, agriculture.

Such changes in the economy have their effect on and are affected by changes in other parts of the society, such as the distribution of the population across the country, opportunities for advancement, and the state of the educational system. An indication of the changing population distribution among the provinces during more or less the same period covered by Table E5 is given by the last column in Table C4 which shows the net gain and loss of native-born Canadians by province. The net loss from Manitoba and Saskatchewan during this time reflects the movement out of agriculture and the large gain in Ontario reflects the increasing importance of secondary manufacturing industries and of commercial and other services. A further change concomitant with increased industrialization is the growth of urbanization, a process which can be seen in Table A15.

Social change takes place over both long and short periods of time. Table E5, which we have been using as an example, covers a relatively short time-span. Others, such as E9, which outlines the changing participation of women in the labour force, span the whole of the present century. The greater the length of time covered by a table, the better the historical perspective it provides on social change.

The collection of social statistics is a large-scale undertaking conducted primarily by government agencies – in Canada, for example, by the Dominion Bureau of Statistics, and by other federal and provincial departments as well. The recording of births, marriages and deaths, of the amount of money paid in wages and salaries to all those at work, of the output during the year of almost every conceivable product, of the movement of capital into and out of the country – all this counting requires an enormous machinery, both human and non-human. No doubt the largest single data-collecting operation in Canada is the census which takes place every ten years. This is an attempt to count all people and families in the country and to collect, at the same time, other information about them, such as their ethnic affiliation, religion, educational level, birth place, occupation, mother tongue and so forth. (So rapidly has social change been taking place in Canada since World War II that a further census asking everyone a limited number of questions has been taken at the mid-points between the main decennial censuses – that is, in 1956 and in 1966.) The census is actually a constitutional requirement for determining the redistribution of seats in the federal House of Commons, but with each census more information has been collected, so that it has gradually become the richest single source of information available about Canadian society. Consequently, the decennial census, from the first in 1871 to the tenth in 1961, has been a very important source for the tables in this volume. Some care is, however, necessary in looking at census tables, particularly those of the 1951 census, when for some purposes Newfoundland, which joined the Confederation in 1949, is excluded. At times, also, Yukon and the Northwest Territories are omitted. These exclusions can on occasion lead to different totals for the same thing.

The census is a total enumeration of everybody in the country and is obviously a very time-consuming and expensive operation, both in the collecting and in the processing of the data included. In social research it is not always necessary to count everybody. Typically, when large populations are being studied it is sufficient to collect the information from only a part, or a sample, of the population. Sampling of representative cross-sections of a population is a highly technical statistical procedure, and statistics based on samples can have a high degree of reliability. One very large sample survey undertaken in Canada every month is the Labour Force Survey based on a sample of 30,000 households. The aim of this survey is a precise estimate of the number of unemployed. Another important sample survey undertaken by the Dominion Bureau of Statistics every few years is one which tries to measure the distribution of income among non-farm families in Canada. The 1960 survey was based on a sample of 8,700 families and individuals.

A large part of the business of collecting statistics is the automatic registration of particular events: births, marriages, deaths, arrests, convictions, hospital admissions and so forth. These registrations being made in many different places across the country, it is important that everyone responsible register the event in the same way and that the registration be complete. Unfortunately, such requirements are not always met. An apparent rise in hospital admission rates may, for example, suggest that people are more ill than formerly, but it may also be an artifact of the way the statistics are collected in that more hospitals have been brought into the registration procedure. There is a need to impose a "quality control" on collecting statistics, especially in a country as widespread as Canada with its ten provincial governments, each of which is responsible for a large proportion of registrations. Particularly since World War II, federal and provincial government officials have been working together to try to maintain and improve the quality of statistics. While there are other sources of statistical materials (welfare agencies, trade associations, educational institutions and the like), governments maintain the most highly developed statistics-collecting operations. It is they who need the information to construct and implement broad economic and social policies.

Earlier it was suggested that statistics which cover different points in time are important for the analysis of social change. This task is often made difficult by the lack of comparable statistics. While there is a reasonable body of statistics on Canadian economic activities going back for some considerable time, there is, generally speaking, a dearth of statistical materials for other social activities which are of interest to the sociologist. The reason is that nobody collected them; or, if they did, they failed to do so consistently or in a uniform fashion. The publication in 1965 of the volume, *Historical Statistics of Canada*[1], was an important event in Canadian social science. Although concerned mostly with economic activities, it nevertheless brought together from a wide variety of sources statistical time series from the nineteenth century on.

Even vital statistics, which describe the most basic changes in the structure of the population, are not available for Canada for the period before 1921. After that year, and in accordance with an agreement between Canada and the provinces, uniform statistical records were kept of births, stillbirths, marriages and deaths. In 1945 a further step towards improvement in registration techniques and procedures and in the quality of vital statistics was taken with the creation of the Vital Statistics Council. Before 1921 vital statistics were estimated from census to census by applying mortality rates and making estimates of

[1] M. C. Urquhart (Ed.), *Historical Statistics of Canada* (Toronto, 1965).

immigration and emigration. Even the population movements into and out of the country, which have been such an important process in Canadian history, have not been recorded with any great care until fairly recently. Statisticians have been able to make some estimates of these movements. Nevertheless, the overall picture of social change which might be provided by statistical time series is limited by the amount of uniform and comparable statistics which are available. The absence of such data is one of the reasons why the historical tables in this volume vary so much in the time periods which they cover.

The ways in which statistics are gathered will themselves be affected by social change. As the importance of social activities or the prevalance of certain social events changes, government administrators stop collecting some statistics and begin collecting others. Or the statistics themselves, once collected, may be arranged in different groups or categories in such a way that they are not comparable with earlier series. Moreover, as our knowledge of social behaviour increases and our theories about it become more sophisticated, it is necessary to construct new statistical materials as the empirical counterparts to new theories. In other words, there are sometimes genuine scientific reasons for breaking up the historical continuity of statistical collections. Those who are responsible for such collections have to solve the problem of conflict between historical comparability and theoretical relevance.

One of the difficulties of analysing social behaviour in quantitative terms is the need for precise definitions, so that all the things being counted together are, in fact, the same. Such precision may seem fastidious to the layman who is accustomed to thinking about social processes in the looser terms of popular speech, but the social scientist wants to measure, and, if he is going to do that with anything approaching accuracy, he must make sure that he is putting the right things into the classifications which he is using. What, for example, is a "labour force" in a modern economy? Does it include males and females? What ages are to be included? Does it include unpaid work in family enterprises? How much work a week must a person do before being included? What about the unemployed? When is a married woman unemployed? In collecting data on the labour force statisticians must decide what to exclude and what to include and then be consistent. Even with vital statistics definitions have to be clearly stated. Births include only infants born alive. Stillbirths are also recorded, but is a stillbirth one of at least 28 weeks or only 20 weeks gestation? Hospitals, too, have to be clearly defined for statistical purposes.

People at work, births, deaths, hospitals are relatively concrete things or events, but social scientists are also concerned with other forms of social behaviour which are much less concrete. How is one to identify and define crime, alcoholism, university enrolment, a student, ethnicity and so forth? Clearly, unless definitions become standardized over time and place, the statistics are not comparable. It would be impossible or misleading to compare different provinces within the country or to compare changes over time if definitions were not the same. Alcoholism is an example. Is it increasing or decreasing? Is it more prevalent in one province than another? Obviously, this is an illness which cannot be clearly defined. Physicians would probably disagree on its diagnosis, and, in addition, there is considerable social stigma attached to it. However, cirrhosis of the liver is a disease caused by alcoholism which is relatively uniformly diagnosed and does not carry a stigma. Consequently, death rates from cirrhosis are the most widely used statistical measures of varying rates of alcoholism.

In most of the tables that follow, the sources from which they are drawn give clear definitions of what is being counted. Occasionally, these have been indicated in the tables or in the relevant parts of the text. It would be impossible to include them all, but the original sources can always be consulted. In fact, anyone interested in studying Canadian society cannot avoid becoming familiar with these sources, since they are a rich field to explore and the tables in this volume are only hints of what they contain.

A Commentary on the Tables

A. DEMOGRAPHIC STRUCTURE

Human society is a collection of people bound together by a set of ordered relationships and sharing common values. Clearly, the size, age and sex composition, and geographic distribution of a society's population will have an important bearing on what the society can do. At the same time, human resources are more than sheer numbers; it is only when members of a society have been trained to take on the many tasks that are necessary to keep the society going that they constitute a human resource in the real sense.

The tables in Section A show how the Canadian population has grown, the various elements that have made it grow, and its geographical distribution. Between the first census in 1871 and the last in 1961 the population of Canada grew from 3.7 million to 18.2 million. This increase has not, however, taken place at a uniform rate. The two periods of very rapid growth, 1901 to 1911 and 1951 to 1961, were also periods of rapid economic development and high levels of immigration. In both decades the proportionate increase was around one-third (A2), while the lowest proportionate increase, about one-tenth, took place during the decade of the 1930's, the time of the great depression.

Population growth has not, then, proceeded at a steady rate, nor has it been uniformly distributed across the country. Different parts have experienced differing rates of growth at different times. These differences can be accounted for by changing economic factors. Thus, in the first years of the century when the West was being opened up, the population of Alberta and Saskatchewan increased by more than 400 per cent. After World War II the provinces of rapid population growth were Alberta, British Columbia and Ontario. The Atlantic Provinces have grown very slowly during the present century.

Demographers speak of the components of population growth, by which they mean natural increase and net migration. The natural increase is the excess of births over deaths, and net migration is the excess of immigrants over emigrants. Table A3 shows how these different components have varied between 1871 and 1961. It is clear that the most important element in Canadian population growth has been natural increase, resulting from high birth rates and low death rates (A4). Between 1951 and 1961 natural increase was 3.1 million, while net migration was 1.0 million (A3). There have, in fact, been decades in Canada's history when net migration has been negative. These have also been periods of low economic activity. It has been estimated by one demographer[1] that, between 1851 and 1950, 7.1 million people arrived in Canada, while 6.6 million left, making the net gain over one hundred years only about half a million.

Falling birth and death rates have been generally characteristic of Western industrial societies. In Canada, between 1851 and 1961, the birth rate fell from an estimated 45 per 1,000 population to 26 per 1,000, while the death rate fell from an estimated 22 to 9 per 1,000 population (A4). In 1960 this drop in the death rate, along with the still relatively high birth rate, resulted in a higher rate of natural increase in Canada than in other countries – for example, the United States and the United Kingdom – at similar stages of economic development (A6).

The fall in the death rate has resulted from a great reduction in infant deaths and in deaths from childhood infections and contagious diseases. There have also been great improvements in public health measures and in immunization programmes. The lowering of death rates, in turn, increases life expectancy, which between 1931 and 1961 has risen from 60.0 years at birth to 68.3 years for males and from 62.1 to 74.2 for females (A7). Thus, a girl born in 1961 could expect to live twelve years longer than her mother born in 1931. The fact that so many people are living longer creates a new interest in aging, not only as a biological process, but also as a social one requiring new roles for older people.

In comparing death rates between provinces, regions or countries, it should be remembered that they will be affected by variations in the age structure of the populations. It is interesting, however, that the differences among the provinces in death

---

[1] N. Keyfitz, "The Growth of the Canadian Population," *Population Studies*, IV (June, 1950).

rates between 1931 and 1961 have moved in the direction of equalization (A5). This would suggest that all provinces have benefited from the improvement in medicine.

The age and sex structure of the population is important because it affects both fertility and mortality – that is, the capacity of the population to reproduce itself and to grow in numbers. Canada has always had a relatively young population, about one-third being under fifteen years of age, except at the 1941 census when that age group was 27.8 per cent, reflecting probably the lower marriage rates and birth rates which prevailed during the depression years of the 1930's (A9). For almost all age groups Canada has an excess of males over females (A8). In the earlier part of the century the excess of males was caused, in part, by the pattern of immigration, which included more men than women. In more recent years, however, family immigration has been much more typical. Demographers have taken various components of the population growth and projected the Canadian population to 1981, at which time they estimate there will be a population of 28.2 million, an increase of over 50 per cent in twenty years (A10).

Marriage seems to have become increasingly popular during the last sixty years in that a smaller proportion of the population, both male and female, was single in 1961 than in 1901 or 1931 (A11). In 1961 three-quarters of the population over 15 years were still single until the age of 24, but four-fifths of the age group 25 to 34 years were married (A12). For men over 15-24 years of age 85.7 per cent were single, but for women the proportion drops to 68 per cent. Throughout the present century a larger proportion of women were widowed, a fact which reflects their greater longevity (A11).

Changes in the distribution of the population among the various provinces and regions have been noted earlier, but undoubtedly the most marked geographic change during the present century has been the shift from a rural to an urban environment. Every census from 1871 to 1961 has shown a steady increase in the proportion of the population in urban areas (A13). In 1961 less than one Canadian in three lived in rural areas. The proportion of the population living in cities of various sizes can be seen in Table A14. In 1901 less than one-tenth of the population lived in cities with a population of

100,000 and over, and three-quarters lived in communities of less than 5,000. In 1961, by contrast, more than one-fifth lived in cities of 100,000 and over. In the interval there was also a substantial increase in the proportion of the population in cities between 10,000 and 100,000.

The most important measure of urbanization is the growth in metropolitan areas – that is, areas in which communities spill over into one another, so that they become one large urban mass. In 1961 almost 45 per cent of the Canadian population lived within these metropolitan areas compared to an estimated 32 per cent in 1941 (A15). Metropolitan areas ranged in size from Montreal and Toronto with 2.1 million and 1.8 million respectively, down to St. John's, Newfoundland, with 91,000.

The major demographic changes during the first sixty years of the present century, shown in Tables A1 to A15, have been responses to both internal and external economic factors. The dominant trend has been to industrialization and urbanization, although periods of slow growth and relative stagnation have, at times, occurred as well. The transition from a rural life based on an economy of primary production, particularly agriculture, to one that is urbanized and industrialized will be traced also in tables in other sections, especially the one dealing with the economy.

B. MARRIAGE AND FAMILY

Because it is affected by cultural values and social practices, human fertility is as much a social as a biological phenomenon. It is checked to some extent by the almost universal acceptance of the idea that reproduction should take place after marriage and that children should be brought up within family units. The definition of suitable marriage partners and the structure of family relationships will, however, vary with different cultures. Within any one culture social and economic factors will also influence the rate and age of marriage, the size of family, and the prevalence of divorce.

In Canada, both males and females were, on the average, marrying earlier in 1961 than in 1921 (B1). In 1921 the average age for males at marriage was 29.9 and for females 25.5, but in 1961 they were 27.7 and 24.7, respectively, thus showing also a decline in the difference in the age of marriage between men and women. Almost without exception the lower average age at marriage is uniform for all provinces. The differences that do exist among them suggest that, in the more industrialized and urbanized provinces, both males and females may be marrying later.

Marriage rates are affected by the age and sex structure of the population, as well as by social factors, such as cultural values and fluctuations in the level of economic activity. The drop in the marriage rate to a low of 6.4 per 1,000 population in 1931 (B2) was, no doubt, brought about by the onset of the depression, and the increase to a high point of 10.6 per 1,000 of population in 1941 probably resulted from the postponed marriages of the depression decade, as well as from the tendency toward earlier marriage during the first years of World War II. Throughout the 1950's there was a return of the marriage rate to what it was in the 1920's, but it is still high considering the low birth rates of the 1930's, which reduced the proportion of those of marrying age in the late 1950's and early 1960's. In fact, the relative size of the age group 15 to 29 years in 1961 was the lowest it had ever been since the census of 1901 – that is, 21 per cent of the total population (A9).

The cultural norm that men marry women younger than themselves is illustrated also in Table B3. For example, in 1961, 15.5 per cent of husbands, but 23 per cent of wives, were less than 30 years old. If the table is read diagonally from top left to lower right, and if the under 20's are excluded, the largest proportions of married couples are made up of husbands and wives in the same age groups, although it should be noted that the table uses both 10-year and 15-year age intervals.

Demographers have given a great deal of attention to falling birth rates in all industrialized societies. For Canada this fall can be seen in A4, but these are very crude fertility rates. More accurate measures of a society's capacity to reproduce itself are the number of children born to women within the reproductive years (i.e., age-specific fertility rates) or the number of women of reproductive years having female children (i.e., the gross reproduction rate). Age-specific fertility rates for Canada from 1931 to 1961 are given in B4. The crude rate is high, having increased from 93.6 per 1,000 women 15 to 49 years in 1931 to

111.5 in 1961. It should not, however, be concluded that there is an overall trend to larger families. The increase in the fertility rates is much greater in the younger age groups (B4 and B5). These differences in fertility among age groups suggest that women are having children more when they are younger and less when they are older. It may be surmised that families are, in fact, being completed when mothers are younger than formerly. This earlier family formation would also seem to be borne out by the decreasing average age of fathers and mothers (B6).

The vast majority of the population live within families and households. Although these two primary groups are typically the same, the census makes a distinction between them (B7 and B8). A family is defined as a husband and wife, without children or with children who have never married, or a parent with one or more children never married, living together in the same dwelling. A household, on the other hand, is defined as any group of persons sharing a common dwelling. Almost 30 per cent of "families" consist of married couples without children living at home (B7 and B9). Where there are children, there are somewhat more families with two children than with any other number. There are proportionately fewer children where the family head is widowed or divorced.

Although everybody knows what a family is, it is always necessary to define it carefully for research purposes. For example, in a sample survey of non-farm family income, families were defined slightly differently (B10), as a group of individuals sharing a common dwelling unit and related by blood, marriage or adoption. The assumption here is that a group of related kin will pool their income resources. In 1961 35.6 per cent of all non-farm families had combined incomes of less than $4,000. The average income was $5,317 and the median, $4,866. The latter means that 50 per cent had less than $4,866 and the other 50 per cent more. Tables of income distribution must be looked at closely to be sure of what they contain. For example, tables based on individual incomes will show a greater proportion at lower-income levels than those based on pooled family income. Table E16, for example, includes unattached individuals with non-farm families and shows 46.1 per cent of income recipients at less than $4,000. It is family income which determines levels of consumption and life chances. Generally, the older the family head, the greater is the average total family income (B10). The census of 1961 showed that the proportion with incomes over $10,000 a year was 0.8 per cent when the head was under 25 years, but 11.1 per cent when the head was between 55 and 64 years. This increasing income with the age of the head of the family derives from the higher earnings of the head himself as he gets older, but also from the fact that other family members will be going out to work as well. When the family head has passed 54 years, the *average* total family income begins to decline. After 65 years the decline is especially marked.

C. MIGRATION

Canada, like the United States and Australia, is a new society which has been built up by large masses of people moving into great open spaces on a vacant continent. Atlhough, as we have seen, net migration has not been nearly as important to Canadian population growth as natural increase, this has resulted from the outflow of people sometimes outnumbering the inflow. At all times some proportion of the population has been foreign-born: 15.6 per cent in 1961, 22.2 per cent in 1931, and 13.0 per cent in 1901 (C1). The higher proportion in 1931 reflected the heavy immigration during the first decade of the century and after World War I. Between 1901 and 1931 immigration actually totalled 4.6 million (A3).

Before World War II more of the foreign-born came from the United Kingdom than from any other country. The declining importance of that country as a source of immigrants can be seen from C1. In 1901 just under 60 per cent of the foreign-born came from the United Kingdom, but that proportion dropped to one-half by 1931 and to only slightly over one-third by 1961.

A changing pattern can also be seen in the distribution of immigrants among the various provinces. In Quebec, according to the 1961 census, 53.9 per cent of the province's foreign-born population had arrived in Canada during the preceding decade (C2). For Ontario the proportion was almost as high (49.1 per cent). In Saskatchewan, on the other hand, over half of the foreign-born population had arrived before 1921, as had 41 per cent of Manitoba's. It is clear (C3) that immigration after World War II went primarily to Quebec (16.4 per cent) and, more especially, to Ontario (55.3 per cent), with the other provinces receiving rather smaller proportions, while the pre-1921 immigration contributed greatly to the settlement of the West.

Throughout the present century Canada has received large numbers of immigrants and has seen large numbers of foreign- and native-born leave as emigrants. It has also experienced a high level of internal migration of native-born Canadians, responding to the push and pull of changing economic conditions. Throughout the whole period the Atlantic provinces have been the great losers in this internal shift of population (C4). Before World War I Quebec and Ontario were also losers, contributing with immigrants from abroad to the building of the West. Subsequently, these two provinces have, in the main, gained in the population exchange. During the off-farm migration of the 1950's Ontario, British Columbia and Alberta gained, while Saskatchewan and Manitoba lost.

D. LANGUAGE, ETHNICITY AND RELIGION

All societies are internally differentiated, and the more developed and complex they are the greater their differentiation. Briefly stated, the basis of differentiation is the social division of labour by which different members of the society perform different tasks or roles in the whole system of activities and relations which contribute to the on-going social order. This condition can be seen most clearly in the occupational and industrial structures of the economic system, although it applies throughout the social system. In other words, the major institutional orders, such as the economic, political and educational systems, perform quite diverse functions, thus contributing to the process of differentiation.

Other aspects of social life also break up the social mass and provide focal points around which social groupings cohere. Language, ethnicity and religion have been important sources of social differentiation throughout Canada's history. At times this differentiation has amounted to a divisiveness so intense as to threaten the coherence and survival of Canadian society.

Everyone in Canada, except an Indian or Eskimo, is required

for census purposes to have a non-Canadian ethnic origin. This origin is determined by the census enumerator asking, "To what ethnic or cultural group did you or your ancestor on the male side belong on coming to this continent?" Ethnicity is then traced through the paternal line, while the maternal line is ignored. There is no official Canadian ethnicity.

Unlike the United States, Canada has adopted a set of values which emphasize these ethnic and religious differences, rather than the "melting pot" values which attempt to minimize such differences in the proces of creating a new ethnicity – a new nation. Canada has always been characterized by dualisms: the historic dualism between French and English Canada, and the dualism which all are expected to feel between their Canadian identity and their identity with the ethnic and cultural origins, mostly European, of their forefathers. Some would argue that these dualisms prevent the emergence of a true Canadian identity, while others would claim that retention of European identities enriches Canadian life. The religious, ethnic and language composition of the population, and the degree to which this has changed, can be seen in Tables D1 to D9.

Although Canadian values emphasize cultural pluralism, there does not seem to be a confusion of tongues. In 1961 almost nine-tenths of the population had English or French as their mother tongue – that is, the language they first learned in childhood and still understand (D1). English was the mother tongue of 58.5 per cent and French of 28.1. Although these proportions have changed little over the last thirty years, there seems to be a tendency for non-English and non-French speaking immigrants to teach their children English rather than French. The increase in those whose mother tongue is Italian reflects the post–World War II immigration, as does the increase between 1951 and 1961 in the proportion whose mother tongue was German. The decline in "All Other" mother tongues between 1931 and 1961 confirms this general assimilation to English on the part of newcomers.

The Dutch, Jews and Italians speak both French and English in greater proportion than do other groups. A much greater proportion of the French than the English speak both official languages. The general pattern, already noted, of all immigrant ethnic groups to assimilate to the English language rather than the French is shown also by the very sizeable proportions of the European ethnic groups who identify English as their mother tongue rather than French or even the language of their own ethnic group (D2). It would seem that the longer the groups are in the country the greater is the likelihood of successive generations teaching their children English. The British have steadfastly declined to become bilingual!

The proportion of British in Canada has been declining throughout the present century from 57.0 per cent in 1901 to 43.8 per cent in 1961 (D3), while the proportion of French has remained much the same except for a slight downward trend in the 1930's, no doubt because of the high European immigration in the preceding 10 years. The Germans have always been third in size among Canada's ethnic groups. In 1901 the Canadian ethnic "mosaic" had scarcely developed. By 1931 it became more evident, and by 1961, 26 per cent of the population were of neither British nor French origin.

Differences in age and sex composition and in marriage and fertility rates among the various groups change the distribution of the groups in the population over time. This changing ethnic composition can be seen from the 1961 distribution of ethnic groups by age (D4). For those under 15 only 41.4 per cent of the population were British, compared to 57.7 per cent of the population 65 and over. The French, on the other hand, made up 33.4 per cent of the under 15's compared to 21.6 per cent of the over 65's. Many other groups contributed more heavily to the younger part of the population than to the older. The Canada of the future is, consequently, likely to become much less "British" than it has been in the past.

The various ethnic groups are also distributed differently in the occupational structure (D5). Generally speaking, the British and the Jews are over-represented in the higher professional and financial occupations and under-represented in the primary and unskilled occupations. The French, on the other hand, are under-represented in the professional and financial group and over-represented in the primary and unskilled jobs. Almost all other groups follow the French pattern. If they are not over-represented in primary and unskilled jobs, they are in agriculture. The groups vary very much also in their proportions in personal service occupations. These data would suggest that ethnicity has become an important characteristic by which people are arranged in the work world. Asian and European immigrants have, for example, been brought into the country at various times to do unskilled work or to settle on farms. They come in at a particular occupational level and tend to remain there, with subsequent immigration reinforcing this pattern. Skilled and professional immigration has, by contrast, been largely from the United Kingdom, thus strengthening the position of the British in the higher-level jobs.

This association of immigration and occupational level helps to create ethno-religious sub-cultures with different value systems. In a society with a high degree of ethnic differentiation, and hence a plurality of sub-cultures, the question arises whether there is a sufficient sharing of a common value system to maintain the coherence of the larger society.

Sub-cultural values and occupational attainment are both, in turn, related to educational experience. In Canada, in 1961, 68.3 per cent of the group 5 to 24 years of age was still in school compared to 53.8 in 1951, but there were considerable differences among ethnic groups (D6). The French had only 64.1 per cent in school in 1961; the Italians, 61.2 per cent; and the Indians and Eskimos, 54.8 per cent. Among the groups with more than the national proportion still in school were Jews (84.8 per cent), Asians (73.6 per cent), and the British (72.3 per cent).

Much of what has been said of ethnic groups can also be applied to religious groups, since they often overlap considerably. The British, for example, make up the major part of the United, Anglican, Presbyterian and Baptist churches, while the French constitute the largest part of the Catholic affiliation, the Germans and Scandinavians of the Lutheran, and the Ukrainians of the Greek Orthodox and the Ukrainian Catholic (D9). Roman Catholics have always been Canada's largest religious group (D7). In 1961 they made up 45.7 per cent of the population. The United Church after its formation became the second largest. As with ethnicities it is interesting to look at the 1961 distribution of religious groups by age (D8). Roman Catholics make up just over half of those under 15, but slightly less than one-third of the population 65 and over. All other religious groups have a smaller proportion in the younger part of the population than in the older. Canada, then, seems to be on a path to becoming increasingly more Catholic and, as we have already seen, less British.

E. THE ECONOMY

The economy is the major institutional order through which a society produces and distributes its material wealth. Some theories hold that it is the most important set of social activities, all others being given their character and shape by the economic conditions and arrangements by which a society lives. Although there are ways in which non-economic factors can assert their primacy over the economic, the economic conditions of any society are obviously basic to its capacity to produce wealth. These conditions include both natural resources and the quality of the labour force. The age and sex composition and educational levels of the labour force are, therefore, key features to analyse in the assessment of a society's productive potential.

One measure of economic output is the Gross National Product. In constant (1949) dollars – that is, adjusted for inflation – the Canadian Gross National Product grew from 7.5 billion in 1931 to 26.5 million in 1961 (E3). In per capita terms the increase was from $729 to $1,452. Over the same period the labour force grew from 3.9 to 6.5 billion, although a somewhat smaller proportion of the total population worked in 1961 than in 1931 (E1). In addition, the work week became shorter. For non-agricultural workers, for example, it fell from 49.6 hours in 1926 to 40.6 hours in 1955 (E4).

The drop in the proportion of the total population at work reflects both a longer time spent in school and earlier retirement. Males and females show quite opposite trends in their participation in the labour force. The proportion of males participating in the labour force fell from 89.6 per cent in 1911 to 77.7 per cent in 1961, while the proportion of females rose from 16.2 per cent to 29.5 per cent. In fact, in 1961 over one-fifth of the married women and over half the single women over 15 years of age were working (E2).

There are several ways, in addition to changes in the Gross National Product, by which to measure the development of the economy. One is to look at the shift out of primary and secondary into tertiary economic activity – that is, from goods-producing to service-producing work. In Canada this shift became very rapid after World War II (E5). In 1963 only 2.9 out of 6.4 million workers were engaged in goods-producing industries. This was about the same number as in 1946 and represented an increase over the seventeen years of only 3 per cent. During the same period, while the labour force as a whole increased by 36 per cent, workers in the service-producing industries increased by 87 per cent. In other words, almost all the new jobs created by the economic expansion over these years went into service-producing activities, including transportation and communication, trade, finance, insurance and real estate, public administration, and business, personal and community services, and recreation. Although there was practically no proportionate increase for goods-producing industry as a whole, its internal components did, however, change sharply. Workers in the primary industries decreased by 40 per cent, a loss which reflected the large-scale movement out of agriculture, while in the secondary manufacturing industries they increased by 44 per cent.

It can be seen from an examination of the changes in the occupational composition of the labour force that, by 1961, only 10 per cent was in agricultural occupations, a drop from 16 per cent in 1951, 25.8 per cent in 1941, and 28.8 per cent in 1931 (E6). Increasing industrialization had brought a shift out of primary occupations into more highly skilled manual and white-collar occupations. Between 1931 and 1961 the proportion of the white-collar component of the labour force rose from 24.4 per cent to 38.6 per cent. Atlhough the proportion in manual occupations remained about the same during this time, there is no doubt that many of these manual jobs required a higher level of skill. This general upgrading of the labour force necessitated by the changes in the occupational structure has placed great demands on educational systems. In Canada, however, a sizeable proportion of this demand for skilled and professional workers has been met, not through the educational systems themselves, but through immigration.

Part of the increase in the white-collar component of the labour force has been the previously suggested very great increase in the number of women workers. In 1901 only 12 per cent of women of labour-force age were actually at work, and they made up only a little more than 13 per cent of the total labour force (E9). By 1961 the corresponding figures were 29.5 and 27.3 per cent. However, it should be noted that labour-force age was defined as 10 years and over in 1901 and as 15 years and over in 1961, so that some portion of the change resulted simply from the altered definition.

Considered separately, the male and female labour force show a different structure (E7). Because many teachers (70.7 per cent) and most nurses (96.8 per cent) were women, over 15 per cent of women workers were in professional and technical occupations in 1961, compared to only 7.5 per cent of male workers. A large proportion (51 per cent) of the female labour force was also in clerical, service and recreational occupations. By contrast, the largest occupational classification for male workers was craftsmen and production process workers (28.5 per cent). In most societies there are fairly clear social norms about appropriate work for men and women. With the growth of industrialized economies women leave their traditional domestic roles in increasing numbers, but in the main they have been restricted to "appropriate" female jobs in the economic system. For example, over one in ten of all women workers in 1961 were stenographers and typists, and they made up 97 per cent of this occupational group (E10). In fact, more than 60 per cent of all women workers were in the ten leading female occupations.

Within the most highly trained professions there are also important male and female differences (E8). In 1961 there were only 116 women professional engineers compared to 42,950 men, and only 328 women lawyers compared to 12,594 men. All modern industrial societies are in increasing competition for professional workers. It is, therefore, probable that, if for no other reason than the requirements of maintaining a complex economy, it will be necessary for women to move more than in the past into professional fields that have been traditionally reserved for men.

The general shift from manual to non-manual occupations which has come with industrialization and which results in an upgrading of the labour force has provided extensive opportunities for upward social mobility, since the recruits to fill this great expansion of higher-level jobs must come from the unskilled classes. These constantly increasing opportunities in industrial societies have prevented them from experiencing the severe social conflict which was predicted by Marx and other nineteenth-century socialist writers. Instead of a large homogeneous mass of unskilled workers at the bottom levels of society, there has, in fact, been a great decrease in the proportion of such workers. Another important factor in alleviating class conflict has been the development of labour unions which have been able, for large numbers of workers, to achieve great gains in wages and working conditions. The structure of organized labour in Canada has been influenced largely by the international unions of the United States. In Canada during World War II there was a substantial increase in the proportion of industrial workers organized into unions, from 18 per cent in 1941 to 28 per cent in 1951. The high point was reached in 1958 when 34.2 per cent of the non-agricultural workers belonged to unions (E11). Since that time there has been a steady decline in the proportion because of the shift in the occupational structure. In 1961 the transportation industries were the most heavily unionized (53 per cent of the workers). For manufacturing occupations the proportion was 39.7 per cent, whereas for workers in trade and commercial occupations the proportion unionized was very low indeed (E12). Traditionally, unions have existed to improve conditions for manual workers, and they have, by and large, neglected or been spurned by white-collar workers. It would seem, then, that if unions are to remain an important social force they will have to devise new methods of recruiting from non-manual occupations.

Opportunities to benefit from the changing structure of occupations which has been briefly sketched depend very much on a person's education. In 1961 60 per cent of those in professional and technical occupations had a university degree, or at least some university education (E13). Professional and technical occupations similarly ranked first in income (E14). There was also a high proportion with some level of higher education in the managerial and proprietary occupations, but this is not a very satisfactory occupational classification, since it includes managers and owners of large enterprises as well as small ones.

If these two components could be separated, the importance of education to getting on would be more clearly demonstrated.

Industrialization also leads to the increasing concentration of economic power, a process by which fewer and fewer producing units are responsible for a larger proportion of the total output of the economy. The primary mode of organizing and controlling productive instruments is the large corporation. In 1962 it took only 84 corporations, each with assets of over $100,000,000 and together making up only 0.3 per cent of the 24,508 reporting, to account for 29 per cent of all the assets of all the corporations reporting, 30 per cent of all their equity capital, 18 per cent of all their Sales, and 32 per cent of all their profits (E17). Companies with assets of over $50,000,000 are still large. These numbered 206, or 0.8 per cent of all corporations reporting, and they accounted for 42 per cent of all the assets, 44 per cent of all the equity, 29 per cent of all the sales and 47 per cent of all the profits.

The economy produces goods and services to be distributed throughout the society according to prevailing values about how this should be done. The unequal distribution of money income has been dealt with earlier and, as suggested, the problems of measuring it are great. Another approach would be to examine the distribution of goods in Canadian households. Advertising in newspapers and magazines can give the erroneous impression of a society of great affluence in which all families have an unlimited range of appliances and gadgetry. It is possible to think of a standard package of household goods which might be enjoyed by a majority of households. Some indication of this standard package is given in Table E15. Surveys of this kind make no judgments about the state of repair of the equipment or whether it is completely paid for. By 1964 it would appear that a hot-air furnace, a refrigerator, a floor polisher, one radio, television and telephone, and one automobile had become a part of the Canadian standard package. Items which had not yet been included were home freezers, automatic dishwashers, clothes dryers, washers, record players and power lawn mowers.

F. GOVERNMENT

Modern political systems have the function of mobilizing the total resources of the society and directing these towards the society's major goals. At times, say during war, these goals may be very clear, but at other times they are usually cast in very general terms, such as working for the greater glory of its god, human progress, social equality, or the elimination of poverty. The idea that governments should play this role of direction and leadership is primarily a development of the twentieth century. In the previous century government was seen as an evil whose activities should be reduced to a very minimum of defence and the enforcement of internal rules. The desire for limited government was not surprising, since there had been centuries of struggle to get rid of tyrannical monarchs and oligarchies and to establish some degree of civil rights and a general condition of freedom.

Modern, complex urban-industrial societies require something more than policemen and soldiers on guard to keep them running properly. As social differentiation becomes more marked, governments increasingly take on an integrating function. Moreover, over the years new ideas have developed about the way in which the resources of the society should be used and their products distributed. These led to demands for the extension of the franchise, so that more and more people participated in the political system as full citizens. In time the attainment of political rights gave rise to claims for social rights, claims which during the twentieth century have become so extensive that they can be implemented only through the activity of the state. In most modern electoral democracies full adult suffrage has been achieved only in the present century, although manhood suffrage had generally been established somewhat earlier. Adult suffrage means in principle that all can participate in the political processes by voting at election time, joining parties and running for office.

The first federal election in Canada based on adult suffrage was in 1921, when 89 per cent of the population was eligible to vote and 70 per cent of those eligible did so (F1). It was also the election which broke up the traditional two-party system, with 29 per cent of the seats and 27 per cent of the vote going to parties other than the Liberal and Conservative, mainly the Progressive Party, which had its strength in the West (F2). In some elections in the earlier years of this century scarcely more than two-fifths of the population were enfranchised, but since 1921 the proportion has been about nine-tenths.

Not all of those who are eligible to vote exercise that right, even though some worked so hard to obtain it. In Canada, over successive elections, at least one-fifth of those eligible have not bothered to vote. The election of 1953, when almost one-third did not vote, was an all-time low in participation since 1896 (F1).

Electoral democracies have different forms of government. Some, like the United Kingdom and Canada, have parliamentary systems in which the party which wins the most seats in the House of Commons forms the government. In Canada it is possible but rare for a party to have the largest proportion of the popular vote, but not to win enough seats to form the government. Table F2 shows how often this has happened since the election of 1896. In that year the Liberals had a slightly smaller portion of the popular vote than the Conservatives (the party with the largest vote), but gained a majority of the parliamentary seats. This or a similar situation recurred on a few occasions, most recently in 1957, when the Conservatives had a smaller popular vote than the Liberals, but a sufficiently greater number of seats to form a minority government. On the other hand, in eleven of the twenty elections between 1896 and 1965 governments have been formed by parties which had less than half the popular vote.

While the extension of the franchise has been one important political development of the twentieth century, a concomitant development, as already noted, has been the much more significant role governments have assumed in the regulation of social and economic life. In part this has been a response to the demands for a stable economy in the post-World War II period in the interest of avoiding the economic instability of the 1930's. Also, with the growth of the welfare state, citizens look increasingly to governments to provide a wide range of social welfare measures, and these expectations have led to much greater government participation. In addition, during and since World War II, there has been a high level of military expenditure. It is not surprising, then, that modern governments have become the largest employers in their countries, creating within the ranks of public administrators entirely new career systems and centres of power. In 1960 employees of the federal government totalled 465,998 or 7.3 per cent of the labour force. A little more than one-quarter of these were in the armed services (F3). Between 1933 and 1960 total expenditures by all levels of government (after eliminating transfers among them) rose from $950 millions to $10,784 millions. Over these years there has also been a change in the pattern of expenditures (F4). A very large proportion of the expenditures of all levels of government goes to social welfare, education and health. Gradually, government has taken over many of the functions previously performed by other institutions, such as the family and the church.

G. EDUCATION

Educational systems can be viewed in two ways. They can be seen as performing the function of training people in sufficient quantity and of sufficient quality for occupational roles in a complex division of labour – that is, as having a manpower function. They can also be seen as doing something for individual persons – developing their talents, widening their horizons, improving their minds, and teaching them about the good life.

With social change in the direction of greater industrialization, educational systems become crucially important for their manpower function. More and more people must be trained to higher levels of skill. Often this is done with considerable cultural lag. It takes time before the need to improve the educational system is realized, and it takes time to transmit to young people the appropriate values about education.

As Canada has become more industrialized, the general educational level of the population has become higher. This can be seen by the increasing proportion of the population staying in school for a longer time, as well as by the higher educational level of those who have left school for the labour force. In 1911, 79.7 per cent of those between 10 and 14 years of age were in school (G1). This proportion has increased steadily since that time, and by 1961 it stood at 97.1 per cent. Quebec and Newfoundland have been slightly behind other provinces in this development.

A better test of the adequacy of an educational system to provide the skills necessary for industrial occupations may be found in the proportion of those 15 to 19 years remaining in school, as well as in the proportion who continue into some form of post-secondary education, particularly university and post-graduate work. Here Canada has not done as well as it might have, although there has been some improvement in recent years. At the threshold of the great industrial expansion after the war, Canada had no more than 40.5 per cent of the age group 15 to 19 in school. Newfoundland had only 38.4 per cent, while British Columbia had 52 per cent (G1). Ontario, which was to be the province of great industrial growth, had only 43.7 per cent. By 1961, however, for the country as a whole the proportion of this age group still in school had risen to 58.5 per cent. Quebec had only one-half at school, while British Columbia had just over two-thirds. Some provinces also showed different proportions of males and females in school. For example, only 46 per cent of Quebec females between 15 and 19 years were in school in 1961, compared to 54 per cent of males. > females

Although education has been considered increasingly as a social right, there have been different ideas about how much of it should be available for all. At one time it seemed sufficient for the state to provide elementary education only. In 1911, as previously mentioned, 79.7 per cent of the 10 to 14 years age group were in school, but only 18.7 per cent of those 15 to 19 years. Even as late as 1931 only one-third of the latter group were in school, and in Quebec the proportion was under one-quarter. The Canadian high school has clearly been very slow to develop into a social institution involving widespread participation on the part of the relevant age group.

This slow development of secondary education can be seen also in the educational levels of the Canadian labour force. At the beginning of the 1950's over one-half of the male labour force had no more than elementary school education and only 9 per cent had some form of post-secondary education. Generally speaking, women workers were better educated than men (G2). This difference is connected with the relatively smaller number of women in the labour force. In addition, for many women who do work there is a direct link between their education and their occupations, some of which, like teaching and nursing, require considerable education. Even in 1961 the proportion of males with only elementary school education was 44 per cent. When education has been slow to develop and when such a large proportion of the parental generation has a low level of education, the family cannot be expected to transmit all of the appropriate values about education, and hence the society at large must assume a more important role in this respect.

Canada is certainly a long way from making university education a social right. There is, of course, a limit to the proportion of any human population who can master the work that is required at the university level. At present, this is thought to be somewhere in the range of one-quarter to one-third, but improved methods of teaching and greater motivation are social variables which could push it up. Clearly, the more developed the industrial economy, the greater its need for highly trained workers. Canada has very far to go in developing its higher talents. In 1962-63 the proportion of those 18 to 24 years enrolled in universities and colleges was 8.0 per cent, a rise from 4.2 per cent in 1951-52, with a considerable, though declining, difference between males and females (G4). Perhaps the 18 to 21 year age group would be a better one against which to measure the adequacy of participation in higher education. In the 1960's the proportion of this age group in universities and colleges was about 12 per cent.

For those receiving a university degree the courses most frequently taken have been in the Arts and Sciences (G5). This holds for both men and women. It is the Faculties of Arts and Science (these have been combined in many Canadian universities) which produce a large number of secondary school teachers. In Law and Medicine the proportion of total degrees given to women is very small. The final test of an educational system is the number of people taking post-graduate training and contributing through research to the store of knowledge. In 1961 only 305 doctorates were awarded compared to 20,240 bachelor's degrees (G5).

Canadians often compare themselves to the United States and frequently assume that they are very similar in social structure and values to their great neighbour. As measured by the educational levels attained by the male labour force, there is, in fact, a considerable gap between the two countries. For example, 14.7 per cent of the U.S. male labour force aged 25 to 34 years have university degrees compared to 6.0 per cent in Canada (G8), and 57.2 per cent of the same age group in the U.S. have completed 4 years of high school compared to 28.2 per cent in Canada. Canada also has a smaller proportion of the age group completing elementary school. Moreover, the fact that sizeable differences exist for the older age group 55 to 64 years as well suggests that there has been a long-lasting difference between the two countries in the evaluation of education.

When only a proportion of those within the appropriate age group are admitted to university or college, there must be some way of allocating the places. One standard might be the ability of students or their parents to pay the costs. However, a society is obviously more likely to maximize its human resources by allocating places on the basis of intellectual capacity regardless of family means. The latter method assumes that students do not encounter financial or other barriers and that, once the most able have identified themselves, they are all adequately motivated. Very rarely do these two conditions apply. In some societies much has been done to remove the costs, but the evidence would suggest that there are differences among groups and sub-cultures in their evaluation of education and in their readiness to postpone immediate gratifications and to endure the long training. In most industrial societies this differential evaluation is associated with class position. Consequently, the social composition of students in universities is skewed towards the middle and upper classes. In Canada, where the cost to the student of higher education has remained quite high, the skew is rather pronounced. In one sample survey of the incomes and expenditures of Canadian university students almost 20 per cent of those in Arts and Science in 1961-62 had fathers who were in professional occupations. By contrast these occupations accounted for only 7.6 per cent of the male labour force (G6). A further 27 per cent had fathers who were owners and proprietors, managers and superintendents compared to 9.9 per cent of the male labour force. At the other end of the class spectrum 10.4 per cent of Arts and Science students had fathers in manufacturing and mechanical occupations compared to 22 per cent of the male labour force. A further example of how class affects educational experience is the fact that the more expensive the university course the greater the proportion of students' parents in higher occupational levels. For example, 29.5 per cent of medical students had fathers who were in professional occupations.

These findings demonstrate a clear relation between the socio-economic position of the family and the educational level of the children. Correspondingly, there is little doubt of a close association between education attained and income subsequently earned: the higher the educational level, the greater the proportion of earners in higher income groups (G7).

H. LEISURE

Industrial economies produce much more with a smaller proportion of the population at work than do less developed ones. The school-leaving age is raised, the retirement age is lowered, and the retired live longer, but the economy is capable of carrying this increased load of dependants. In adition, as we have seen, the working day and working week are reduced, giving greatly increased scope for leisure and recreation. Some people despair at the way in which modern societies amuse themselves, but they often overlook the fact that mass spectator sport, much of it more bloodthirsty than anything known in modern times, goes back to antiquity. In addition, a new capacity for leisure activity comes with literacy, a condition that goes with modern societies and their highly developed educational systems. Earlier, this capacity was available to relatively few. At the same time, with mass literacy and technological change in the media of communication, leisure-time activities have undergone a considerable commercialization.

There are very few statistical data which go back far enough for us to trace any changing pattern of leisure activities. In 1951 there was a relatively large number of motion picture theatres, but with the advent of television this number declined, though this was at the same time accompanied by an increase in outdoor drive-in picture theatres. Consequently, in 1961 there were fewer regular motion picture theatres than in 1931 (H1). On the other hand, the number of establishments devoted to bowling, golf, horse racing and riding has increased substantially during the same period.

In 1931 amusement and recreation establishments absorbed 21 per cent of all the money spent on services, but by 1961, despite a fivefold increase in receipts, the proportion was only 8.4 per cent (H1). Other types of service and of amusement had, in the interval, established their claim on consumer expenditures. Our earlier look at the standard package of Canadian households would suggest that television and radio, as well as the family automobile, are obviously important sources of recreation. The first of these did not exist and the last two were only beginning to be available in 1931.

The consumption of beer, wine and spirits also contributes to recreation. (We shall see later how these can contribute to deviant behaviour as well.) All beer, wine and spirits consumed in Canada in 1961 equalled 1.59 gallons of absolute alcohol per capita. Beer contributed the most (62 per cent), while spirits made up 31 per cent and wine 7 per cent (H2). Spirits were more important to drinkers in Nova Scotia, New Brunswick and British Columbia than in other provinces. Beer was the most popular of the alcoholic drinks in Quebec. In total amount Canadian consumption of alcohol does not appear to be unlike that of the United States and the United Kingdom, although the form in which it is consumed differs among the three. In the heavy wine-drinking countries of Italy and France the consumption is much higher, even though it includes relatively smaller amounts of beer or spirits.

Reading occupies at least some of the leisure time of most Canadians. Daily newspaper circulation increased greatly between 1921 and 1963, although the actual number of newspapers remained much the same (H3). A small investment in plant was sufficient for newspapers with a daily circulation of a few thousand copies, but as the size of cities increased, a much greater investment was required to print daily runs of over one hundred thousand copies. Modern daily newspapers are clearly big businesses. The number of weekly newspapers has fluctuated throughout the forty-year period. Canadians buy vast quantities of magazines and periodicals, most of them from the United States. *Reader's Digest* in 1959 had a combined Canadian circulation in English and French of about one million per issue, and

Time had a weekly circulation of 210,000. The pulp magazines, ranging from comics to romance stories, had a total annual circulation of more than 30 million.

In 1962 there were 874 public libraries with an annual circulation of over 65 million books (H4). Almost half the available books and periodicals in libraries are in Ontario, as is over half the circulation from public libraries. Quebec is least well served by public library facilities.

For the more serious, some leisure time is taken up with various forms of adult education. In 1962 over 200,000 Canadians were registered part-time in diploma or degree courses at some level of the educational system. Almost four million attended public lectures and film showings (H5).

I. DEVIANT BEHAVIOUR

Human behaviour is regulated by social norms. These norms are the ideas which the members of the society carry around in their heads about what is appropriate behaviour in various circumstances and what is the correct way of acting out social roles. There are, for example, clearly defined norms about how the role of father, wife, teacher, or soldier should be performed. Some norms are required by the wider society, while others might be required only by certain sub-groups. The former, for example, might insist upon monogamous marriage, but accept divorce, while one of the latter might demand indissoluble monogamy. Norms range from the more serious ones, which govern fundamental social relationships, to the more trivial rules of etiquette. They are embodied in religious and moral teachings, in the law and in social conventions. In many situations there is, of course, a permissible range of deviation from the norms; indeed, this is necessary to accommodate the very great differences in human personality. Violations of norms bring sanctions against offenders, ranging from the simple lessening of social interaction with the offender to outright expulsion from the group, and even death. Rewarding and punishing behaviour according to whether it conforms to or departs from the norms is one of the ways in which a society achieves a degree of integration.

It is the task of the socializing agencies, family, school,

church and so forth, to produce individual personalities which can operate within the permissible range of behaviour. Deviant behaviour, which can take many forms, results from the failure of these agencies to create the type of personality which is consistent with its norms. The major types of deviance with which the wider society is concerned are criminal behaviour, mental illness, alcoholism, and drug addiction. Most large-scale industrial societies have institutionalized the mechanisms of punishment through judicial, penal and rehabilitation systems.

Criminal behaviour ranges from the less serious offences punished by fines or probation to the more serious ones punished by jail sentences. The former are typically dealt with by magistrates or justices of the peace by summary convictions; the latter, the indictable offences, by superior courts. In Canada in 1961, there were over three million summary convictions, almost all of which were punished by fines (I1); about three-fifths of these were parking offences. In the same year there were 38,679 persons convicted of indictable offences, the largest proportion of which, about one-half, were crimes against property, mainly theft or breaking and entering but without any use of violence (I2). About half of all indictable convictions brought jail sentences, and about one-sixth, almost all of which were for crimes against property, resulted in suspended sentences with probation. Tables I1 and I2 provide an overall picture of deviant behaviour which has been dealt with by the police and successfully prosecuted in the courts. They do not include juvenile delinquency. It is also well to remember that some criminal behaviour goes unseen and that an additional amount which is known to the police does not lead to arrests and convictions.

Over 90 per cent of all convictions for indictable offences are of men, and, for men, the rates of conviction are highest between 16 and 24 years of age. Crime rates fall very considerably in older age groups (I3). For convicted females, the rates are also higher in the earlier than in the later years. Rates are higher, for both men and women, in urban than in rural areas. The highest rate of conviction, 23.1 per 1,000 population, is of urban males, 16 to 19 years of age. It is often assumed that there is a higher rate of criminality among immigrants than among the native-born. However, this is not the case. The rate for the Canadian-born is 2.18 per 1,000 population, while for those born in European countries, for example, it is 1.41 (I4).

As we have seen, the rate of convictions is highest for the post-adolescent and early adult age groups. These young offenders in many cases have previous records as juveniles. In areas of large cities where the primary group relationships of family and gang fail to transmit the appropriate social norms of the wider society, the delinquent sub-culture constitutes a criminal nursery.

In Canada in 1961 40 per cent of the 15,215 juvenile offences leading to convictions in juvenile courts were for theft and having in possession, and a further 22 per cent were for breaking and entering (I5). Crimes against the person were relatively infrequent. Only a very small proportion of juvenile offences, 13 per cent in 1961, led to incarceration. Over half were put on probation, some in care of their parents, but most under the supervision of the courts. Returning to an earlier point, close to three-quarters of all juvenile offenders had both parents born in Canada (I6). About 18 per cent had both parents born outside the country, while the remainder had one parent only born outside. It is not possible with these data to establish precisely rates of juvenile delinquency based on parental birthplace. About nine-tenths of convictions for juvenile offences are of boys, the great majority of whom are still in elementary school. There would seem to be an association between slow progress through school and delinquent behaviour (I7).

Deviant behaviour has many roots. Among these are the strains of living in a highly differentiated society, where the roles which the individual is required to assume may often be incompatible with one another – for example, the role of mother conflicting with a professional or work role. There are also the strains imposed by a conflict in values that may be experienced in moving from one sub-culture to another as the individual pursues his career or becomes upwardly mobile. At times these conflicts and strains are too great and result in the disintegration of personality and in mental illness. It is often suggested that the rates of mental illness keep rising as the society becomes more industrialized. This certainly sounds plausible, and generally the data on mental illness seem to bear it out, but modern societies have much greater facilities for dealing with these illnesses than formerly, and modern medicine has much-improved diagnostic procedures. It is, therefore, difficult to know whether the rates are, in fact, higher than they were, and, if so, by how much.

In Canada the rate of patients in mental hospitals has increased from 317 per 100,000 population in 1932 to 365 in 1961 (I9). The rate appears to have fallen since 1951, but this may reflect differences in admissions policy and in therapy, as well as the possibility that facilities did not keep pace with the need. This conclusion would seem to be borne out by the increasing rate, for both men and women, of first admissions to mental hospitals between 1932 and 1962 (I10).

Another type of casualty from the strains of modern social life is the alcoholic. As we have seen earlier, Canadians on the average consume about the same amount of alcohol as people in the United States and the United Kingdom. Clearly, drinking itself is not a violation of social norms, despite the efforts of temperance organizations to define it as such. However, some personalities become increasingly dependent on alcohol to keep going and, eventually, they consume to the point of incapacitating themselves for any kind of social role. At this point their behaviour is defined as deviant. As with mental illness, it is difficult to tell how much of the apparent increase in alcoholism can be attributed to improvements in detection and in therapeutic facilities. Moreover, attitudes about alcoholism have probably led to serious under-reporting of its prevalence. In recent years cirrhosis of the liver—an illness to which alcoholism eventually leads – has come to be regarded as the best single index which is free from social values or unreliable diagnosis. It would seem that death rates from cirrhosis have fluctuated between 1901 and 1961, although there has been a marked increase in cirrhosis deaths as a proportion of all deaths (I11).

Narcotic drug addiction is also a form of deviant behaviour, but it is much less prevalent because of the greater cost and difficulty of obtaining drugs as compared with alcohol. Of the 3,576 recorded drug addicts in Canada in 1962 over half were in British Columbia.

Provinces vary a great deal in amount and type of deviant behaviour. Table I13 is a master table of rates of indictable offences, juvenile delinquency, divorce, illegitimate births, suicides and alcoholism. It also shows the rank of every province on the various forms of deviance. The especially striking point is that British Columbia ranks first on four of these forms and second on the other two. Much sociological research would have to be done to interpret adequately these sometimes considerable differences among the provinces.

J. ILLNESS AND MORTALITY

We have noted in the section on demographic structure how the death rate has fallen as the society has become more industrialized. Much of this achievement must be attributed to great advances in medicine, but public health policies and the extension of hospital facilities have also contributed. The question of the continued expansion of these facilities through social policies and medical care programmes constitutes one of the great debates in North America in the middle of the twentieth century. The notion that good health is a social right like education is becoming an increasingly affirmed value in Canada. Per capita expenditures on almost all forms of medical service increased sharply between 1951 and 1961 (J1). Similarly, a greater proportion of the gross national expenditure has been going into health services than formerly. Hospital admission rates and days of care per 1,000 of the population have also been on the increase (J2).

Perhaps the most outstanding medical success has been the fall in the infant mortality rate from an average of 84 per 1,000 live births for the years 1921 to 1925 to 26.3 in 1963 (J4). Equally spectacular has been the decline in the death rates from infectious and communicable diseases, which were once the major causes of death (J5). This fall has resulted in increased longevity into the middle and later years, so that heart disease and cancer have now become the major causes of deaths. However, once again, some of the increase in rate from these two illnesses has probably resulted from improved diagnostic techniques.

CONCLUDING NOTE

If there is any dominant trend illustrated by these tables, it is the emergence of Canada as a modern industrial society and the concomitant shift to urbanization. These processes have created increasing differentiation within the various institutional systems, but they also appear to be producing an homogenization of Canadian society, at least in the sense that the country as a whole is experiencing the influence of industrialization. As this condition continues, the differences among the provinces and regions may be expected to decline. It may also be predicted that there will, in the future, be a greater equalization of the rates of many of the phenomena we have been examining. Quite possibly, even the major differences between the English-speaking and the French-speaking in Canada will lessen greatly as French Canada becomes more industrialized. The two groups will, no doubt, retain their own language, but they will share an urban-industrial culture which will make them, in many respects, very much alike.

TABLES ON

CANADIAN SOCIETY

A:

DEMOGRAPHIC
STRUCTURE

TABLE A1

Area and Population by Province, 1961

| | Area in Square Miles | | | | Population | | |
	Land	Water	Total	%	Number	Per Sq. Mile	%
Newfoundland	143,045	13,140	156,185	4.1	457,853	3.20	2.5
Prince Edward Island	2,184	–	2,184	.1	104,629	47.91	.6
Nova Scotia	20,402	1,023	21,425	.6	737,007	36.12	4.0
New Brunswick	27,835	519	28,354	.7	597,936	21.48	3.3
Quebec	523,860	71,000	594,860	15.4	5,259,211	10.04	28.8
Ontario	344,092	68,490	412,582	10.7	6,236,092	18.12	34.2
Manitoba	211,775	39,225	251,000	6.5	921,686	4.35	5.1
Saskatchewan	220,182	31,518	251,700	6.5	925,181	4.20	5.1
Alberta	248,800	6,485	255,285	6.6	1,331,944	5.35	7.3
British Columbia	359,276	6,976	366,255	9.5	1,629,082	4.53	8.9
Yukon	205,349	1,730	207,076	5.4	14,628	.07	.1
Northwest Territories	1,253,438	51,465	1,304,903	33.9	22,998	.02	.1
Canada	3,560,238	291,571	3,851,809	100.0	18,238,247	5.12	100.0

Source: Dominion Bureau of Statistics, *Canada Year Book, 1963-64* (Ottawa, 1964), pp. 2 and 160.

TABLE A2

Population by Province, and Percentage Change, 1901-1961

	Population 1901	Percentage Change 1901-1911	1911-1921	1921-1931	1931-1941	1941-1951	1951-1961	1901-1961	Population 1961
Newfoundland	–	–	–	–	–	–	26.7	–	457,853
Prince Edward Island	103,259	–9.2	–5.5	–.7	8.0	3.6	6.3	1.3	104,629
Nova Scotia	459,574	7.1	6.4	–2.1	12.7	11.2	14.7	62.5	737,007
New Brunswick	331,120	6.3	10.2	5.2	12.0	12.7	15.9	80.6	597,936
Quebec	1,648,898	21.6	17.7	21.8	15.9	21.7	29.7	219.0	5,259,211
Ontario	2,182,947	15.8	16.1	17.0	10.4	21.4	35.6	185.6	6,236,092
Manitoba	255,211	80.8	32.2	14.8	4.2	6.4	18.7	261.5	921,686
Saskatchewan	91,279	439.5	53.8	21.7	–2.8	–7.2	11.2	908.6	925,181
Alberta	73,022	412.6	57.2	24.3	8.8	18.0	41.8	1,724.0	1,331,944
British Columbia	178,657	119.7	33.7	32.3	17.8	42.5	39.8	812.3	1,629,082
Yukon	27,219	–68.7	–51.2	1.8	16.2	85.1	60.8	–46.7	14,628
Northwest Territories	20,129	–67.7	25.1	14.4	29.1	33.1	43.7	14.3	22,998
Canada	5,371,315	34.2	21.9	18.1	10.9	21.8[1]	30.2	239.6	18,238,247

[1]Includes Newfoundland in 1951, but not in 1941.

Source: *Census of Canada, 1961*, vol. 7.1-1, Introduction, table I.

TABLE A3

Factors of Population Growth, 1871-1961

	Population at Beginning of Decade (000s)	Births[1] (000s)	Deaths[1] (000s)	Natural Increase (000s)	Immigration[2] (000s)	Emigration (000s)	Net Migration (000s)
1871-1881	3,689	1,477	754	723	353	440	-87
1881-1891	4,325	1,538	824	714	903	1,109	-206
1891-1901	4,833	1,546	828	718	326	506	-180
1901-1911	5,371	1,931	811	1,120	1,759	1,043	716
1911-1921	7,207	2,338	988[3]	1,350	1,612	1,381	231
1921-1931	8,788	2,415	1,055	1,360	1,203	974	229
1931-1941	10,377	2,294	1,072	1,222	150	242	-92
1941-1951	11,507	3,184	1,214[4]	1,970	548	379	169
1951-1961[5]	14,009	4,468	1,320	3,148	1,543	462	1,081
1961[5]	18,238						

[1]Births and deaths for periods from 1871-1921 inferred by applying mortality rates to population figures at each census.
[2]Immigration during census years divided into January-May and June-December in proportions of 5/12 to 7/12.
[3]Allows for 120,000 deaths due to World War I and influenza epidemic.
[4]Allows for 36,000 deaths due to World War II.
[5]Includes Newfoundland.

Sources: Dominion Bureau of Statistics, Canadian Vital Statistics Trends, 1921-1954 (Ottawa, 1956), tables 1 and 2; and Census of Canada, 1961, vol. 7.1-1, Introduction, table III.

TABLE A4

*Estimated Rates of Birth, Death and Natural Increase,
1851-1921*

	Birth Rate[1]	Death Rate[1]	Natural Increase[2]
1851-61	45	22	23
1861-71	40	21	19
1871-81	37	19	18
1881-91	34	18	16
1891-1901	30	16	14
1901-11	31	13	18
1911-21	29	13	16
1961 (actual)	26	9	17

[1]Estimated average annual rate per 1000 population for intercensal years.
[2]Excess of birth rate over death rate.

Source: Dominion Bureau of Statistics, *Canada Year Book 1963-64* (Ottawa, 1964), pp. 227, 237 and 247.

TABLE A5

Annual Live Birth and Death Rates[1] By Province, 1931-1961

	1931		1941		1951		1961	
	Birth Rate	Death Rate	Birth Rate	Death Rate	Birth Rate	Death Rate	Birth Rate	Death Rate
Newfoundland	23.3	13.4	27.3	12.5	32.5	8.3	34.1	6.6
Prince Edward Island	21.3	10.4	21.6	11.9	27.1	9.2	27.1	9.3
Nova Scotia	22.6	11.6	24.1	12.0	26.6	9.0	26.3	8.3
New Brunswick	26.5	11.4	26.8	11.3	31.2	9.4	27.7	7.9
Quebec	29.1	12.0	26.8	10.3	29.8	8.6	26.1	7.0
Ontario	20.2	10.4	19.1	10.4	25.0	9.6	25.3	8.2
Manitoba	20.5	7.6	20.3	8.9	25.7	8.7	25.3	8.0
Saskatchewan	23.1	6.6	20.6	7.2	26.1	7.7	25.9	7.7
Alberta	23.6	7.2	21.7	8.0	28.8	7.6	29.2	6.7
British Columbia	15.0	8.8	18.4	10.4	24.1	10.0	23.7	8.8
Yukon	10.0	16.5	14.4	13.4	38.0	9.4	38.1	6.4
Northwest Territories	15.7	11.8	26.3	25.6	40.6	17.8	48.6	11.4
Canada	23.2	10.2	22.4	10.1	27.2	9.0	26.1	7.7

[1]Rates per 1000 population. The rate of natural increase for each year would be the excess of the birth rate over the death rate.

Source: Dominion Bureau of Statistics, *Vital Statistics, 1962* (Ottawa, 1964), pp. 97 and 122.

TABLE A6

Crude Birth and Death Rates and Rate of Natural Increase for Selected Countries, 1960

Country	Birth Rate[1]	Death Rate[1]	Natural Increase[2]
Canada	26.7	7.8	18.9
United States	23.7	9.5	14.2
United Kingdom	17.5	11.5	6.0
Australia	22.4	8.6	13.8
France	18.0	11.4	6.6
Sweden	13.7	10.0	3.7
Japan	17.2	7.6	9.6
Argentina	22.5*	8.2*	14.3*
Mexico	46.0	11.5	34.5

[1]Per 1,000 of all ages.
[2]The rate of natural increase is the excess of the birth rate over the death rate.
*Preliminary or estimated figures.

Source: *Statistical Year Book, 1962* (United Nations), tables 3 and 4. Copyright, United Nations, 1967. Reproduced by permission.

TABLE A7

Expectation of Life at Birth by Sex, 1931 – 1961

	Male	*Female*
1931	60.00	62.10
1941	62.96	66.30
1951	66.30	70.83
1961	68.35	74.17

Source: Dominion Bureau of Statistics, *Vital Statistics, 1962* (Ottawa, 1964), p. 64, table AA.

TABLE A8

Number of Males per 1,000 Females by Age Group, 1901 – 1961

	Males per 1,000 Females			
Age Group	*1901*[1]	*1921*[1]	*1941*[1]	*1961*
Under 15 years	1027	1018	1025	1046
15-29 years	1034	1004	1015	1018
30-44 years	1083	1157	1067	1005
45-64 years	1083	1159	1144	1037
65 years and over	1050	1047	1037	940
Total	1050	1064	1053	1022

[1]Excluding Newfoundland.

Source: *Census of Canada 1961*, vol. 7.1-4, tabular section, table 2.

TABLE A9

Age Composition of Population, 1901 – 1961

Numerical Distribution

Age Group	1901[1]	1921[1]	1941[1]	1961
Under 15 years	1,846,583	3,023,351	3,198,551	6,191,922
15-29 years	1,502,088	2,206,539	3,119,451	3,825,502
30-44 years	999,234	1,817,546	2,279,945	3,661,695
45-64 years	752,209	1,320,269	2,140,893	3,167,974
65 years and over	271,201	420,244	767,815	1,391,154
Total	5,371,315	8,787,949	11,506,655	18,238,247

Percentage Distribution

Age Group	1901[1]	1921[1]	1941[1]	1961
Under 15 years	34.4	34.4	27.8	33.9
15-29 years	28.0	25.1	27.1	21.0
30-44 years	18.6	20.7	19.8	20.1
45-64 years	14.0	15.0	18.6	17.4
65 years and over	5.0	4.8	6.7	7.6
Total	100.0	100.0	100.0	100.0

[1]Excluding Newfoundland.

Source: *Census of Canada, 1961*, vol. 7.1.4, tabular section, table 2.

TABLE A10

Projection to 1981 of Population by Age Group

Age Group	1961 Actual	1981 Projected[1]	Per cent Increase
Under 5	2,256,401	3,577,000	58.5
5-9	2,079,522	3,139,700	51.0
10-14	1,855,999	2,717,300	46.4
15-19	1,432,559	2,427,800	69.5
20-24	1,183,646	2,313,800	96.3
25-29	1,209,297	2,167,700	79.3
30-44	3,661,695	4,784,700	30.7
45-65	3,167,974	4,735,000	49.5
Over 65	1,391,154	2,383,700	71.3
Total	18,238,247	28,246,700	54.9

[1]Assumes annual net immigration of 50,000.

Sources: *Census of Canada, 1961*, vol. 1.2-3, table 1, and *Report of Royal Commission on Health Services* (Ottawa, 1964), vol. 1, table 4-4.

TABLE A11

Population by Marital Status and Sex, 1901, 1931, 1961

	1901[1]	1931[1]	1961
	Males		
Single	63.5	59.2	54.0
Under 15 years	34.0	30.9	34.3
15 years and over	29.5	28.3	19.6
Married	33.8	38.0	43.6
Widowed	2.7	2.8	2.2
Divorced	–	0.1	0.2
	Females		
Single	59.7	55.4	48.8
Under 15 years	34.8	32.4	33.5
15 years and over	24.9	23.0	15.3
Married	34.5	38.7	44.4
Widowed	5.8	5.8	6.4
Divorced	–	0.1	0.3
	Total		
Single	61.7	57.4	51.4
Under 15 years	34.4	31.6	34.0
15 years and over	27.3	25.7	17.5
Married	34.1	38.3	44.0
Widowed	4.2	4.2	4.3
Divorced	–	0.1	0.3

[1]Excluding Newfoundland.

Source: *Census of Canada, 1961*, vol. 1.2-4, Introduction.

TABLE A12

Population 15 Years of Age and over by Marital Status, Age Group and Sex, 1961

(Percentages)

Males

Age Group	Single	Married	Widowed	Divorced	Total
15-24	85.7	14.3	*	*	100
25-34	23.3	76.3	0.1	0.3	100
35-44	12.0	86.9	0.6	0.5	100
45-54	10.5	87.1	1.8	0.6	100
55-64	11.4	82.6	5.4	0.6	100
65-69	11.0	77.5	11.1	0.5	100
70 and over	10.6	63.6	25.5	0.3	100
All ages 15 and over	29.9	66.4	3.3	0.4	100

Females

Age Group	Single	Married	Widowed	Divorced	Total
15-24	68.0	31.9	0.1	0.1	100
25-34	12.9	86.0	0.6	0.5	100
35-44	9.1	87.8	2.4	0.8	100
45-54	9.9	81.6	7.5	0.9	100
55-64	10.3	69.2	19.8	0.6	100
65-69	10.1	55.3	34.2	0.4	100
70 and over	10.2	33.8	55.9	0.2	100
All ages 15 and over	23.0	66.8	9.7	0.5	100

Total

Age Group	Single	Married	Widowed	Divorced	Total
15-24	76.9	23.0	0.1	*	100
25-34	18.2	81.0	0.4	0.4	100
35-44	10.5	87.3	1.5	0.6	100
45-54	10.2	84.4	4.6	0.8	100
55-64	10.9	76.0	12.5	0.6	100
65-69	10.5	66.2	22.8	0.4	100
70 and over	10.4	48.1	41.3	0.2	100
All ages 15 and over	26.5	66.6	6.5	0.4	100

*Less than 0.05%.

Source: *Census of Canada, 1961*, vol. 1.3-1, Introduction.

TABLE A13

Rural Population as a Percentage of Total Population, 1871-1961

1871	1881	1891	1901	1911	1921	1931	1941	1951(a)[1]	1951(b)	1961
80.4	74.3	68.2	62.5	54.6	50.5	46.3	45.7	43.3	38.4	30.4

[1]Until 1941 the census definition of rural was "unincorporated area." In 1951 this definition was changed to places with less than 1,000 population. For 1951 (a) is the earlier definition and (b) the later one.

Source: *Census of Canada, 1951*, vol. 1, tables 13 and 15, and *Census of Canada, 1961*, vol. 7.1-2, Introduction, table II.

TABLE A14

Population of Cities, Towns and Villages over 1000 by Size, 1901-1961

Per cent of Total Population

Year	Total	100,000 & over	30,000-99,999	10,000-29,999	5,000-9,999	1,000-4,999
1901	34.8	8.9	6.4	4.1	5.3	10.1
1911	41.7	15.0	6.8	6.4	4.5	9.1
1921	45.3	18.9	5.6	7.7	4.4	8.7
1931	49.7	22.4	6.7	8.2	4.4	8.0
1941	50.9	23.0	8.1	7.5	4.4	7.9
1951[1]	53.6	23.3	8.2	8.8	5.1	8.2
1961[1]	58.3	22.8	12.1	10.8	5.1	7.5

[1]Including Newfoundland from 1951.

Source: *Census of Canada, 1961*, vol. 7.1-2, Introduction, table VI.

TABLE A15

Metropolitan Areas, 1941-1961

	No. of Areas	Total Metropolitan[1] Population	Per Cent of Canadian Population
1941[2]	12	3,715,000	32.2
1951	15	5,263,383	37.5
1961	17	8,163,986	44.7

1961 Census Metropolitan Areas

	Total Population
Montreal	2,109,509
Toronto	1,824,481
Vancouver	790,165
Winnipeg	475,989
Ottawa	429,750
Hamilton	395,189
Quebec	357,568
Edmonton	337,568
Calgary	279,062
Windsor	193,365
Halifax	183,946
London	181,283
Kitchener	154,864
Victoria	154,152
Sudbury	110,694
Saint John	95,563
St. John's	90,838
TOTAL	8,163,986

[1]Metropolitan areas, as defined for the census, are groups of urban communities which are in close economic, geographic and social relationship.
[2]Estimate only because of boundary changes.

Source: *Census of Canada, 1961*, vol. 7.1-2, Introduction, pp. 14-17.

B:

**MARRIAGE
AND FAMILY**

TABLE B1

Average Age at Marriage by Sex, Canada and Provinces, 1921-1961

	Male					Female				
	1921	1931	1941	1951	1961	1921	1931	1941	1951	1961
Newfoundland	*	*	*	27.2	26.1	*	*	*	23.9	22.8
Prince Edward Island	31.0	29.2	28.9	28.6	26.6	26.9	24.9	25.2	25.0	23.6
Nova Scotia	29.6	28.9	28.0	28.1	26.6	25.4	24.4	24.6	24.5	23.6
New Brunswick	29.4	29.3	28.3	27.8	26.5	25.0	24.5	24.6	24.1	23.6
Quebec	*	29.1	29.2	28.1	27.5	*	25.5	25.9	25.3	24.8
Ontario	29.7	28.8	28.5	28.3	27.8	25.9	24.9	25.2	25.4	24.9
Manitoba	29.9	29.9	29.1	28.6	27.7	25.3	24.8	25.2	25.2	24.7
Saskatchewan	29.9	28.8	28.7	28.2	27.0	24.7	23.4	24.4	24.3	23.7
Alberta	30.6	29.3	29.0	28.2	27.6	25.4	24.0	24.5	24.6	24.4
British Columbia	32.3	31.3	30.4	30.2	29.5	27.4	26.4	26.5	26.9	26.4
Yukon	*	*	*	28.6	31.6	*	*	*	25.7	28.2
Northwest Territories	*	*	*	27.0	27.3	*	*	*	23.8	24.4
Canada	29.9	29.2	28.9	28.3	27.7	25.5	24.9	25.1	25.3	24.7

*Not available.

Source: Dominion Bureau of Statistics, *Vital Statistics, 1961* (Ottawa, 1963), p. 219, table M2.

TABLE B2

Marriage and Divorce Rates,[1] Canada and Provinces, 1921-1961

	Marriage					Divorce				
	1921	1931	1941	1951	1961	1921[2]	1931	1941	1951	1961
Newfoundland	5.7	5.6	8.7	7.0	7.2	*	*	*	.011	.013
Prince Edward Island	5.8	5.6	7.1	5.9	6.0	*	.011	.011	.102	.076
Nova Scotia	6.8	6.6	11.4	7.9	7.2	.066	.070	.118	.291	.332
New Brunswick	8.4	6.2	10.8	8.5	7.5	.038	.049	.190	.302	.324
Quebec	7.9	5.8	9.8	8.8	6.8	.004	.013	.014	.071	.066
Ontario	8.5	6.9	11.4	9.8	7.1	.035	.027	.251	.459	.439
Manitoba	8.7	7.0	11.4	9.5	7.1	.147	.134	.332	.465	.339
Saskatchewan	6.7	6.2	7.9	8.2	6.6	.053	.060	.163	.272	.271
Alberta	7.9	7.0	10.6	9.9	7.9	.177	.214	.391	.627	.780
British Columbia	7.4	5.6	11.9	9.7	6.7	.249	.300	.745	1.149	.858
Canada	7.9	6.4	10.6	9.2	7.0	.060	.067	.214	.376	.360

[1]Per 1,000 population.
[2]Average for 1921-1925.
*Not available.

Sources: Dominion Bureau of Statistics, *Canadian Vital Statistics Trends, 1921-54* (Ottawa, 1956), p. 45 and *Vital Statistics, 1961* (Ottawa, 1963), pp. 218 and 226.

TABLE B3

Husbands and Wives by Their Ages, 1961

Age of Husband	Age of Wife					
	Under 20 years	20-29 years	30-44 years	45-64 years	Over 64 years	Total
			Percentages			
Under 20 years	0.1	0.04	>0.01	>0.01	>0.01	0.2
20-29 years	1.3	13.0	0.9	0.01	>0.01	15.3
30-44 years	0.07	8.3	29.9	1.2	0.01	39.4
45-64 years	0.01	0.1	9.6	23.9	0.5	34.1
Over 64 years	>0.01	0.01	0.1	4.4	6.5	11.0
Total	1.5	21.5	40.5	29.5	7.0	100.0

Source: *Census of Canada, 1961*, vol. 2.1-11, table 95.

TABLE B4

Age-Specific Fertility Rates,[1] 1931-1961[2]

Age Group	1931	1941	1951	1961
15-19 years	29.9	30.7	48.1	58.2
20-24 years	137.1	138.4	188.7	233.6
25-29 years	175.1	159.8	198.8	219.2
30-34 years	145.3	122.3	144.5	144.9
35-39 years	103.1	80.0	86.5	81.1
40-44 years	44.0	31.6	30.9	28.5
45-49 years	5.5	3.7	3.1	2.4
Crude rate[3]	93.6	86.6	109.2	111.5

[1]Number of live births per 1,000 women in the age group.
[2]Excluding Newfoundland for all dates and Yukon and Northwest Territories prior to 1951.
[3]Per 1,000 women 15-49 years.

Source: Dominion Bureau of Statistics, *Vital Statistics, 1961* (Ottawa, 1963), p. 99.

TABLE B5

Age-Specific Marital Fertility Rates,[1] 1931-1961[2]

Age Group	1931	1941	1951	1961
15-19 years	485.0	453.1	498.5	541.2
20-24 years	357.6	340.2	350.4	374.4
25-29 years	257.7	237.8	248.1	255.6
30-34 years	180.9	158.3	168.7	161.4
35-39 years	123.1	99.1	100.6	89.9
40-44 years	52.5	38.9	36.6	32.1
45-49 years	6.5	4.5	3.7	2.8
Crude rate[3]	160.9	149.3	158.9	152.9

[1]Number of live births per 1,000 married women in the age group.
[2]Excluding Newfoundland for all dates and Yukon and Northwest Territories prior to 1951.
[3]Per 1,000 married women 15-49 years.

Source: Dominion Bureau of Statistics, *Vital Statistics, 1961* (Ottawa, 1963), p. 102.

TABLE B6

Births[1] by Age of Parents, 1931-1961

Age of Mother	1931	1941	1951	1961
		Year of Birth		
Under 20 years	5.4	5.8	5.6	7.3
20-24 years	25.1	27.4	27.1	29.3
25-29 years	27.8	30.4	31.0	28.4
30-34 years	21.0	20.2	20.8	19.9
35-39 years	14.4	11.6	11.6	11.4
40-44 years	5.6	4.1	3.5	3.5
45-49 years	0.6	0.4	0.3	0.3
50 years and over	–	–	–	–
Total	100.0	100.0	100.0	100.0
Average Age of Mother	29.2	28.5	28.4	28.1

Age of Father	1931	1941	1951	1961
		Year of Birth		
Under 20 years	0.4	0.5	0.8	1.1
20-24 years	11.2	12.2	14.6	17.2
25-29 years	24.8	28.2	29.0	29.8
30-34 years	24.1	25.9	24.7	24.9
35-39 years	18.9	17.4	16.9	15.5
40-44 years	12.3	9.3	8.9	7.5
45-49 years	5.7	4.3	3.5	3.0
50 years and over	2.6	2.3	1.6	1.2
Total	100.0	100.0	100.0	100.0
Average Age of Father	33.6	32.7	32.1	31.4

[1]Legitimate live births excluding Newfoundland and, prior to 1961, Yukon and Northwest Territories.

Source: Dominion Bureau of Statistics, *Vital Statistics, 1961* (Ottawa, 1963), p. 23.

TABLE B7

Persons per Family,[1] 1951, 1956, and 1961

Number of People in Family	1951[2]	1956[2]	1961[2]
		Percentages	
2	31.2	30.3	28.9
3	24.0	22.0	20.7
4	20.0	20.5	20.6
5	11.0	12.3	13.4
6	5.8	6.6	7.5
7 and over	8.0	8.3	8.9
Total	100.0	100.0	100.0
Number of Families	3,282,445	3,705,607	4,140,384

[1]A family consists of a husband and wife, without children or with children who have never married, or a parent with one or more children never married, living together in the same dwelling.
[2]Excluding Yukon and Northwest Territories as well as military camps and institutions.

Source: Dominion Bureau of Statistics, *Estimates of Families in Canada, 1962* (Ottawa, 1963), table 1.

TABLE B8

Persons per Household,[1] *1941-1961*

Number of People in Household	1941[2]	1951[2]	1961[2]
		Percentages	
1	7.1	7.4	9.3
2	21.6	20.9	22.2
3	21.1	20.2	17.8
4	17.9	18.9	18.4
5	12.2	12.9	13.3
6-7	12.4	12.5	12.7
8-9	4.8	4.5	4.2
10 and over	2.9	2.7	2.1
Total	100.0	100.0	100.0
Number of Households	1,960,167	3,409,284	4,554,736

[1]A household as defined in the census consists of a person or group of persons occupying one dwelling. It usually consists of a family group with or without lodgers, employees, etc. Every person is a member of some household and the number of households is equal to the number of dwellings. A dwelling is defined as a structurally separate set of living quarters with a private entrance either from outside the building or from a common hall, lobby, vestibule or stairway inside.

[2]Excluding Newfoundland before 1951 and Yukon and Northwest Territorie before 1961.

Sources: *Census of Canada, 1941*, vol. 5, Table 17, and *Census of Canada, 1961* vol. 2.1-1, Introduction.

TABLE B9

Distribution of Families by Marital Status of Head and Number of Children[1] at Home, 1961

	Marital Status							
	Married		Widowed		Divorced		Single	
No. of Children	No.	%	No.	%	No.	%	No.	%
0	1,117,559	28.6	97,454	45.6	758	4.8	1,022	11.0
1	768,655	19.7	55,837	26.1	8,378	53.6	5,814	62.3
2	821,457	21.0	28,296	13.2	4,154	26.6	1,289	13.8
3-4	843,206	21.6	22,505	10.6	2,039	13.0	851	9.1
5 and over	357,948	9.1	9,565	4.5	307	2.0	350	3.8
Total	3,908,825	100.0	213,657	100.0	15,636	100.0	9,326	100.0

[1]Includes step-children, adopted children, and wards under 21 years of age.

Source: *Census of Canada, 1961*, vol. 2.1-7, table 73.

TABLE B10

Percentage Distribution of Non-farm Families[1] by Income Groups and Age of Head, 1961

	All Families	24 and under	25-34	35-44	45-54	55-64	65 and over
					Age of Head		
Under 2,000	11.2	14.1	6.2	5.6	7.3	12.9	36.2
2000-3999	24.4	38.5	26.1	20.8	20.8	25.5	29.6
4000-5999	31.6	32.5	40.4	35.6	29.7	25.5	16.4
6000-7999	18.3	11.1	18.1	22.6	20.8	16.5	9.4
8000-9999	7.9	3.0	5.7	9.2	11.2	8.5	5.0
10,000 and over	6.5	0.8	3.5	6.4	10.1	11.1	3.5
Total	100.0	100.0	100.0	100.0	100.0	100.0	100.0
Average Income	$5,317	4,038	5,057	5,737	5,985	5,809	3,737
Median Income	$4,866	3,895	4,797	5,313	5,400	4,826	2,809

[1]In this table a family is a group of individuals sharing a common dwelling unit and related by blood, marriage or adoption. Income includes income from all sources.

Source: Dominion Bureau of Statistics, *Distribution of Non-Farm Income in Canada by Size, 1961* (Ottawa, 1964), table 9.

C:

IMMIGRATION

TABLE C1

Population by Country of Birth, 1901, 1931 and 1961

	1901	1931	1961	
	%	%	Number (000's)	%
Canada	87.0	77.8	15,394	84.4
United Kingdom	7.5	11.0	970	5.3
United States	2.4	3.3	284	1.6
Other Commonwealth	0.3	0.4	48	0.3
European Countries	2.3	6.9	1,468	8.0
Asian Countries	0.4	0.6	58	0.3
Other	–	–	17	0.1
Total	100	100	18,239	100

Source: *Census of Canada, 1961*, vol. 1.2-7, Introduction and table 48.

TABLE C2

Foreign-born Population by Period of Immigration and Province, 1961

	Before 1921	1921-1930	1931-1940	1941-1950	1951-1961[1]	Total
Newfoundland	12.7	8.9	5.4	26.4	46.5	100.0
Prince Edward Island	24.2	14.9	7.3	18.6	35.1	100.0
Nova Scotia	28.6	14.6	6.3	16.2	34.4	100.0
New Brunswick	27.9	17.2	6.2	17.5	31.2	100.0
Quebec	19.2	12.0	3.7	11.3	53.9	100.0
Ontario	19.5	14.7	3.1	13.6	49.1	100.0
Manitoba	41.3	18.5	2.5	10.3	27.4	100.0
Saskatchewan	57.3	20.5	2.1	6.1	14.0	100.0
Alberta	35.0	19.1	2.9	9.6	33.3	100.0
British Columbia	37.3	17.0	2.7	9.9	33.2	100.0
Yukon and Northwest Territories	13.6	14.0	4.2	11.2	57.1	100.0
Canada	27.1	15.6	3.1	11.8	42.3	100.0

[1]First five months only of 1961.

Source. *Census of Canada, 1961*, vol. 1.2-8, Introduction and table 58.

TABLE C3

Post-World War II[1] Immigrants by Province, 1961

	No.	*%*
Ontario	833,303	55.3
Quebec	247,762	16.4
British Columbia	177,544	11.8
Alberta	121,559	8.1
Manitoba	62,498	4.1
Saskatchewan	28,993	1.9
Nova Scotia	16,172	1.1
New Brunswick	10,450	0.7
Newfoundland	4,236	0.3
Yukon	1,724	>0.1
Prince Edward Island	1,488	<0.1
Northwest Territories	1,387	<0.1
Canada	1,507,116	100.0

[1]January, 1946 to June, 1961.

Source: Department of Citizenship and Immigration, *The Basic 1961 Census Data on Immigration and Citizenship* (Mimeo) (Ottawa, 1963), p. 17.

TABLE C4

Internal Migration of Native-Born,[1] 1901-1961

	Net gain or loss of population in each period (in hundreds of persons) due to internal migration of Native-born Canadians					
	1901-1911	1911-1921	1921-1931	1931-1941	1941-1951	1951-1961
Prince Edward Island	−57	−30	+8	−13	−56	−71
Nova Scotia	−129	−63	−96	+48	−274	−342
New Brunswick	−84	−5	−64	−70	−288	−263
Quebec	−240	−146	+241	+263	−108	+99
Ontario	−1473	−27	+514	+1003	+1543	+1069
Manitoba	+160	−185	−316	−338	−575	−354
Saskatchewan	⎫ +1849	+80	−418	−1110	−1507	−935
Alberta	⎭	+204	−135	−299	−94	+277
British Columbia	411	+163	+302	+513	+1317	+509
Yukon and Northwest Territories	−116	+10	+8	+3	+42	+11

[1]Those born or living in Newfoundland are excluded from the table for comparability before and after 1951.

Sources: K. Buckley, "Historical Estimates of Internal Migration in Canada," in E. F. Beach and J. C. Weldon (eds.), *Conference on Statistics 1960* (Toronto, 1962), p. 10, table 3, reprinted by permission of the University of Toronto Press; and *Census of Canada, 1961*, vol. 1.2-7.

D:

LANGUAGE,
ETHNICITY
AND RELIGION

TABLE D1

Mother Tongue[1] of Population, 1931-1961

	1931	1941	1951	1961
		Percentages		
English	57.0	56.4	59.1	58.5
French	27.3	29.2	29.0	28.1
German	3.5	2.8	2.4	3.1
Ukrainian	2.4	2.7	2.5	2.0
Italian	0.8	0.7	0.7	1.9
All Others[2]	9.0	8.2	6.3	6.4
Total	100.0	100.0	100.0	100.0

[1]The language a person first learned in childhood and still understands.
[2]All less than 1 per cent in 1961.

Source: *Census of Canada, 1961*, vol. 1.2-9, Introduction.

TABLE D2

Official Language and Mother Tongue by Ethnic Group, 1961

Ethnic Group	Official Language				Mother Tongue[1]			Other
	English only	French only	French and English	Neither English nor French	English	French	Language of Ethnic Group	
British	95.5	0.4	4.0	0.1	98.6	1.0	0.1	0.3
French	8.6	61.2	30.1	0.2	10.0	89.6	—	0.4
German	95.7	0.5	2.6	1.3	59.0	0.8	39.4	0.8
Ukrainian	94.6	0.2	2.6	2.5	33.9	0.3	64.4	1.4
Italian	65.2	6.8	10.6	17.4	22.2	3.7	73.6	0.5
Dutch	95.3	0.2	2.9	1.6	51.8	0.3	37.6	10.3
Scandinavian	97.4	0.3	2.1	0.2	69.7	0.6	28.8	0.9
Polish	91.3	0.7	5.5	2.5	40.4	0.9	45.5	13.2
Jewish	79.9	0.5	18.4	1.3	57.9	1.3	33.6	7.3
Russian	90.3	0.5	6.5	2.7	46.4	0.7	29.8	23.1
Asian	80.9	1.3	6.6	11.2	30.0	2.4	54.2	13.4
Native Indian and Eskimo	76.6	2.3	1.8	19.2	26.7	1.7	71.4	0.2
Canada	67.4	19.1	12.2	1.3	58.5	28.1	10.9	2.6

[1] The language a person first learned in childhood and still understands.

Source: *Census of Canada, 1961*, vol. 1.3-10.

TABLE D3

Distribution of Population by Ethnic Group,[1] 1901, 1931 and 1961

Ethnic Group	1901 Number (000's)	%	1931 Number (000's)	%	1961 Number (000's)	%
British	3,063	57.0	5,381	51.9	7,997	43.8
French	1,649	30.7	2,298	28.2	5,540	30.4
German	310	5.8	474	4.6	1,049	5.8
Ukrainian	6	0.1	225	2.2	473	2.6
Italian	11	0.2	98	0.9	450	2.5
Dutch	34	0.6	149	1.4	430	2.4
Scandinavian	31	0.6	228	2.2	387	2.1
Polish	6	0.1	146	1.4	324	1.8
Jewish	16	0.3	157	1.5	173	1.0
Russian	20	0.4	88	0.8	119	0.7
All Other European	24	0.4	261	2.5	711	3.9
Asian	24	0.4	85	0.8	122	0.7
Native Indian and Eskimo	128	2.4	129	1.2	220	1.2
Other and not stated	49	0.9	29	0.3	243	1.3
Total	5,371	100	10,377	100	18,238	100

[1]Traced through the father. In 1961 the census question was, "To what ethnic or cultural group did you or your ancestor (on the male side) belong on coming to this continent?" In previous censuses the question was based on language and physical characteristics.

Source: *Census of Canada, 1961,* vol. 1.2-5, table 34.

TABLE D4

Ethnic Groups by Age,[1] 1961

Ethnic Group	All Ages	Under 15	15-44	45-64	65 and over
			Percentages		
British	43.8	41.4	41.6	47.9	57.7
French	30.4	33.4	31.2	26.4	21.6
German	5.8	5.6	6.2	5.4	4.7
Ukrainian	2.6	2.4	2.7	2.8	2.1
Italian	2.5	2.5	3.0	1.8	1.1
Dutch	2.4	2.7	2.4	2.0	1.5
Scandinavian	2.1	2.0	2.1	2.3	2.4
Polish	1.8	1.7	1.8	2.2	1.3
Jewish	1.0	0.8	0.9	1.4	1.0
Russian	0.7	0.6	0.6	0.8	0.8
All Other European	3.9	3.3	4.3	4.5	3.1
Asian	0.7	0.6	0.7	0.6	0.9
Native Indian and Eskimo	1.2	1.7	1.1	0.7	0.7
Other and not stated	1.3	1.4	1.4	1.2	1.2
Total	100	100	100	100	100

[1]For definition see note 1, D3.

Source: *Census of Canada, 1961*, vol. 1.3-2, Introduction.

TABLE 13

Selected Ethnic Origins and Occupational Classes, Male Labour Force, 1931, 1951 and 1961

Over- and Under-Representation[1] in Occupation by Ethnic Group

Occupational Class	British	French	German	Italian	Jewish	Dutch	Scandinavian	East European	Other European	Asian	Indian and Eskimo	Total Male Labour Force
1931												
Professional & Financial	+1.6	−0.8	−2.2	−3.3	+2.2	−1.1	−2.9	−3.9	−4.4	−4.3	−4.5	4.8
Clerical	+1.5	−0.8	−2.2	−2.5	+0.1	−1.9	−2.7	−3.4	−3.5	−3.2	−3.7	3.8
Personal Service	−0.3	−0.3	−1.2	+2.1	−1.2	−1.5	−1.5	−1.1	−1.7	+27.8	−3.1	3.5
Primary & Unskilled	−4.6	+3.3	−5.3	+26.1	−14.5	−4.8	+1.4	+12.4	+35.8	+10.2	+45.3	17.7
Agriculture	−3.0	+0.1	+21.1	−27.6	−32.4	+18.5	+19.8	+14.5	−5.8	−20.9	−4.9	34.0
1951												
Professional & Financial	+1.6	−1.5	−2.2	−3.1	+4.2	−1.7	−2.1	−2.9	−2.4	−2.8	−5.2	5.9
Clerical	+1.6	−0.8	−2.5	−1.7	0.0	−2.4	−2.8	−2.8	−2.5	−2.9	−5.2	5.9
Personal Service	−0.3	−0.2	−1.2	+2.0	−1.4	−1.2	−1.0	+0.6	+2.0	+23.9	−0.6	3.4
Primary & Unskilled	−2.2	+3.0	−3.7	+9.6	−11.5	−1.7	+0.5	+2.3	+5.7	−1.9	+47.0	13.3
Agriculture	−3.2	−0.3	+19.1	−14.7	−18.7	+17.3	+14.7	+11.2	+3.4	−8.7	−7.8	19.4
1961												
Professional & Financial	+2.0	−1.9	−1.8	−5.2	+7.4	−0.9	−1.9	−1.2	−1.1	+1.7	−7.5	8.6
Clerical	+1.3	−0.2	−1.8	−3.2	−0.1	−1.7	−2.4	−1.7	−2.0	−1.5	−5.9	6.9
Personal Service	−0.9	−0.2	−0.7	+2.9	−2.4	−0.5	−1.1	+0.9	+5.1	+19.1	+1.3	4.3
Primary & Unskilled	−2.3	+2.8	−2.1	+11.5	−8.9	−2.0	−0.2	0.0	+1.8	−3.6	+34.7	10.0
Agriculture	−1.5	−1.4	+8.8	−9.5	−11.7	+10.3	+10.6	+6.9	+0.6	−6.5	+6.9	12.2

[1]The figures in the table show the difference, expressed in percentage points, between a given ethnic group's representation in a particular occupational class and that of the total male labour force, as given in the last column.

Source: John Porter, *The Vertical Mosaic* (Toronto, 1965), p. 87; reprinted by permission of the University of Toronto Press.

TABLE D6

Males 5-24 Years Old In School by Ethnic Origin, 1951 and 1961

	British	French	German	Italian	Jewish	Dutch	Scandi- navian	All Other European	Asian	Indian and Eskimo	Percent of Total Age Group in School
1951	56.8	50.5	53.8	45.9	64.9	53.2	56.9	53.5	61.3	41.3	53.8
1961	72.3	64.1	65.6	61.2	84.8	67.0	69.1	70.4	73.6	54.8	68.3

Source: John Porter, *The Vertical Mosaic* (Toronto, 1965), p. 89; reprinted by permission of the University of Toronto Press.

TABLE D7

Religious Denominations, 1901-1961

	1901		1921		1931		1961	
	Number (000's)	%	Number (000's)	%	Number (000's)	%	Number (000's)	%
Roman Catholic	2,239	41.7	3,399	38.7	4,103	39.5	8,343	45.7
United Church	–	–	–	–	2,021	19.5	3,664	20.1
Anglican	690	12.8	1,411	16.1	1,639	15.8	2,409	13.2
Presbyterian	848	15.8	1,412	16.1	872	8.4	819	4.5
Lutheran	94	1.8	287	3.3	395	3.8	663	3.6
Baptist	319	5.9	422	4.8	444	4.3	594	3.3
Greek Orthodox	16	0.3	170	1.9	103	1.0	240	1.3
Jewish	16	0.3	125	1.4	156	1.5	254	1.4
Methodist	925	17.2	1,161	13.2	–	–	–	–
Others	224	4.2	401	4.5	644	6.2	1,252	6.9
Total	5,371	100	8,788	100	10,377	100	18,238	100

Source: *Census of Canada, 1961*, vol. 1.2-6, Introduction and table 41.

TABLE D8

Religious Denominations by Age, 1961

	All Ages	Under 15	15-44	45-64	65 and over
Roman Catholic	45.7	50.2	47.2	39.6	32.2
United Church	20.1	19.5	19.7	21.3	22.5
Anglican	13.2	12.0	12.7	14.5	18.2
Presbyterian	4.5	3.4	4.1	5.9	8.3
Lutheran	3.6	3.1	3.8	4.2	3.7
Baptist	3.3	3.0	3.1	3.6	4.4
Jewish	1.4	1.1	1.3	2.1	1.5
Greek Orthodox	1.3	0.9	1.4	1.7	1.5
Ukrainian Catholic	1.0	0.8	1.0	1.4	1.2
All Others[1]	5.8	5.9	5.6	5.7	6.5
Total	100.0	100.0	100.0	100.0	100.0

[1]All other religious denominations had less than 1 per cent of the population in 1961.

Source: *Census of Canada, 1961*, vol. 1.3-3, Introduction.

TABLE D9

Ethnic Composition of Religious Groups, 1961

	British	French	German	Ukrainian	Italian	Dutch	Scandinavian	Polish	Other	Total
Roman Catholic	17.0	63.7	3.1	1.0	5.0	0.9	0.3	2.5	6.5	100.0
United Church	77.9	2.4	5.1	1.6	0.3	2.8	3.1	0.7	6.1	100.0
Anglican	84.3	2.5	2.8	0.8	0.3	1.3	1.5	0.5	6.0	100.0
Presbyterian	84.6	2.0	3.2	0.7	0.3	2.1	1.4	0.4	5.3	100.0
Lutheran	10.0	1.1	44.2	1.0	0.2	1.5	22.3	1.6	18.1	100.0
Baptist	73.0	2.8	8.9	1.0	0.3	3.4	2.0	0.7	7.9	100.0
Greek Orthodox	1.1	0.3	0.5	49.7	0.1	0.1	0.1	4.1	44.0	100.0
Ukrainian Catholic	1.9	0.9	0.6	83.1	0.2	0.1	0.2	5.6	7.4	100.0

Source: *Census of Canada, 1961*, vol. 1.3-8, Introduction.

E:

THE ECONOMY

TABLE E1

Population in the Labour Force, 1911, 1931 and 1961

	1911	1931	1961
	Number (000's)		
Total Population	7,191	10,363	18,200
Male	3,812	5,367	9,198
Female	3,379	4,996	9,002
Population 15 years and over	4,818	7,086	12,023
Male	2,612	3,710	6,039
Female	2,206	3,376	5,984
Labour Force	2,698	3,908	6,458
Male	2,341	3,245	4,694
Female	357	663	1,764
Labour Force as Percent of	Percentages		
Total Population	37.5	37.7	35.5
Male	61.4	60.5	51.0
Female	10.6	13.3	19.6
Labour Force as Percent of			
Population 15 years and over	56.0	55.1	53.7
Male	89.6	87.5	77.7
Female	16.2	19.6	29.5

Source: *Census of Canada, 1961*, vol. 3.1-1, table 1.

TABLE E2

Population and Labour Force by Sex and Marital Status, 1961

	Single	Married	Widowed and Divorced	Total
Population 15 years and over	3,191,206	8,024,304	830,815	12,046,325
Labour Force	1,878,932	4,366,482	226,436	6,471,850
Male Population 15 years and over	1,811,473	4,019,725	221,604	6,052,802
Male Labour Force	1,131,665	3,487,341	86,512	4,705,518
Labour Force as Percent of Male Population[1]	62.5	86.8	39.0	77.7
Female Population 15 years and over	1,379,733	4,004,579	609,211	5,993,523
Female Labour Force	747,267	879,141	139,924	1,766,332
Labour Force as Percent of Female Population[1]	54.2	22.0	23.0	29.5

[1] 15 years and over.

Source: *Census of Canada, 1961*, vol. 1.3-1, Introduction; vol. 3.1-13, table 18.

TABLE E3

Growth of Gross National Product, 1931-1961

	1931	1941	1951	1961
Current Dollars				
Total in Millions	4,699	8,328	21,170	37,421
$ per capita	453	724	1,511	2,052
Constant (1949) Dollars				
Total in Millions	7,567	12,486	18,547	26,487
$ per capita	729	1,085	1,324	1,452

Source: Dominion Bureau of Statistics, *Canada Year Book, 1963-64* (Ottawa, 1964), p. 1016.

TABLE E4

Average Hours Worked by Persons with Jobs, 1926-1955

	All Workers	Non-Agricultural Workers
1926	55.0	49.6
1930	53.0	48.1
1935	50.2	44.6
1940	52.3	47.9
1945	48.2	44.3
1950	44.8	42.9
1955	43.0	40.6

Source: Based on material from *Historical Statistics of Canada*, M. C. Urquhart, Editor, K. A. H. Buckley, Assistant Editor (Toronto, 1965), p. 105; reprinted by permission of the Macmillan Company of Canada Limited.

TABLE E5

Changes in Employment by Industry, 1946-1963

| | Number of Persons Employed | | Amount of Change | |
| | 1946[1] | 1963 | Number | Percentage |
	(000's)		(000's)	
Goods Producing	2,809	2,883	74	+1
Primary	1,371	819	–552	–40
Secondary	1,438	2,064	626	+44
Service Producing	1,858	3,482	1,624	+87
Transportation and Communication	344	455	111	+32
Public Utilities	33	85	52	+158
Trade	573	1,019	446	+78
Finance, Insurance, Real Estate	124	254	130	+105
Other Services	784	1,669	885	+113
All Industries	4,666	6,365	1,699	+36

[1]Excluding Newfoundland.

Source: Economic Council of Canada, *First Annual Review* (Ottawa, 1964), p. 155.

TABLE E6

Labour Force[1] by Occupational Group, 1931-1961

Occupational Group	1931	1941	1951	1961
		Percentages		
White Collar	24.4	25.2	32.5	38.6
Managerial and Proprietary	5.6	5.4	7.5	7.9
Professional	6.1	6.7	7.4	10.0
Clerical	6.6	7.2	10.9	12.9
Commercial and Financial	6.1	5.9	6.7	7.8
Manual	33.8	33.4	37.6	34.9
Manufacturing and Mechanical	11.5	16.0	17.4	16.4
Construction	4.7	4.7	5.6	5.3
Labourers[2]	11.3	6.3	6.7	5.4
Transportation and Communication	6.3	6.4	7.9	7.8
Service	9.3	10.5	8.6	10.8
Personal	8.3	9.3	7.3	9.3
Protective	1.0	1.2	1.3	1.5
Primary	32.5	30.6	20.1	13.1
Agriculture	28.8	25.8	15.9	10.2
Fishing and Hunting	1.2	1.2	1.0	0.6
Logging	1.0	1.9	1.9	1.3
Mining	1.5	1.7	1.3	1.0
Not Stated in Census	–	0.3	1.2	2.6
	100.0	100.0	100.0	100.0
All Occupations, Number (000's)	3,922	4,196	5,215	6,342

[1] 1931-1951, 14 years of age and over; 1961, 15 years of age and over. Includes Newfoundland in 1951 and 1961, but excludes Yukon and Northwest Territories for all years.
[2] Except in agriculture, fishing, logging and mining.

Source: Department of Labour, *Occupational Trends in Canada, 1931 to 1961* (Ottawa, 1963), table 1.

TABLE E7

Persons in Labour Force, 15 Years of Age and Over, by Occupational Group and Sex, 1961

Occupational Group	Male Number	Male %	Female Number	Female %	Total Number	Total %
Professional and technical	356,578	7.5	272,333	15.3	628,911	9.7
Managerial and proprietary	481,379	10.2	57,661	3.2	539,040	8.3
Clerical	324,811	6.9	509,345	28.7	834,156	12.8
Sales	263,229	5.6	147,486	8.3	410,715	6.3
Craftsmen and production process workers	1,354,594	28.5	205,189	11.5	1,559,783	23.9
Service and recreation	400,399	8.5	395,948	22.2	796,347	12.2
Transport and communication	354,736	7.5	37,968	2.1	392,704	6.0
Miners, quarrymen and related workers	65,119	1.4	22	*	65,141	1.0
Loggers and related workers	78,826	1.7	117	*	78,943	1.2
Fishermen, trappers and hunters	35,648	0.8	274	*	35,922	0.6
Labourers	294,059	6.2	20,943	1.2	315,002	4.8
Farmers and farm workers	573,098	12.1	75,868	4.3	648,966	10.0
Seeking work for the first time	24,253	0.5	14,253	0.8	38,506	0.6
Occupation not stated	123,042	2.6	43,178	2.4	166,220	2.6
Total	4,729,771	100.0	1,780,585	100.0	6,510,356	100.0

*Less than 0.1%

Sources: *Census of Canada, 1961*, vol. 3.1-3, table 6; vol. 3.3-13, table 13.

TABLE E8

Professional Labour Force, by Type of Occupation and Sex, 1961

Occupational Group	Male		Female	
	No.	%	No.	%
Teachers	63,194	17.7	125,978	46.3
Professional engineers	42,950	12.0	116	0.1
Health professionals	42,098	11.8	96,201	35.3
Accountants and auditors	29,121	8.2	1,549	0.5
Religious professionals	23,982	6.7	9,733	3.6
Artists, writers and musicians	19,934	5.6	11,818	4.3
Law professionals	12,594	3.5	328	0.1
Physical scientists	10,471	2.9	591	0.2
Biologists and agricultural professionals	5,576	1.6	360	0.1
Social welfare workers	5,071	1.4	5,784	2.1
Architects	2,874	0.8	66	>0.1
Librarians	630	0.2	2,809	1.0
Dietitians	66	>0.1	1,849	0.7
Other professionals	98,017	27.4	15,151	5.6
Total	356,578	100.0	272,333	100.0

Source: *Census of Canada, 1961,* vol. 3.1-3, table 6.

TABLE E9

Women in the Labour Force,[1] 1901-1961

Year	Of Working Age[2] (000's)	In Labour Force No. (000's)	%	Percentage of Total Labour Force
1901	1,982	238	12.0	13.3
1911	2,552	365	14.3	13.4
1921	2,843	489	17.2	15.5
1931	3,481	665	19.1	17.0
1941	4,133	834	20.2	18.5
1951	4,933	1,164	23.6	22.0
1961	5,984	1,764	29.5	27.3

[1]Excluding Yukon and Northwest Territories.
[2]1901 and 1911, 10 years and over; 1921 to 1951, 14 years and over; 1961, 15 years and over.

Source: Department of Labour, *Women at Work in Canada* (Ottawa, 1964), table 1.

TABLE E10

Ten Leading Female Occupations, 1961

Occupation	Number	Percentage of Female Labour Force	Women as percentage of all workers
Stenographers and Typists	209,410	11.9	96.8
Clerical Occupations	165,613	9.4	51.2
Sales Clerks	133,234	7.6	58.0
Maids and Related Service Workers	120,161	6.8	88.1
School Teachers	118,594	6.7	70.7
Bookkeepers and Cashiers	98,663	5.6	62.6
Nurses	81,868	4.6	96.8
Farm Labourers	66,081	3.7	29.7
Waitresses	61,802	3.5	78.6
Sewers and Sewing Machine Operators	50,592	2.9	90.5
Total 10 occupations	1,106,018	62.7	66.3
Total Female Labour Force	1,763,862	100.0	27.3

Source: Department of Labour, *Women at Work in Canada* (Ottawa, 1964), table 11.

TABLE E11

Union Membership in Non-Agricultural Industries, 1911-1961

	Total Non-agricultural Paid Workers	Union Membership	Percent Unionized
1911		133,000	
1921	1,956,000	313,000	16.0
1931	2,028,000	311,000	15.3
1941	2,566,000	462,000	18.0
1951[1]	3,625,000	1,029,000	28.4
1954	3,754,000	1,268,000	33.8
1958	4,250,000	1,454,000	34.2
1959	4,375,000	1,459,000	33.3
1961	4,578,000	1,447,000	31.6
1963	4,867,000	1,449,000	29.8
1965	5,343,000	1,589,000	29.7

[1]Includes Newfoundland for the first time.

Source: Department of Labour, *Labour Organizations in Canada* (Ottawa, 1965), table 1.

TABLE E12

Union Membership by Industry, 1961

Industry	Number in Labour Force	Union Membership	Per cent of Industry Unionized
Transportation, storage, and communication	532,782	282,300	53.0
Logging	108,580	55,800	51.4
Public utilities	70,504	35,400	50.2
Mining	121,702	59,800	49.1
Manufacturing	1,404,865	558,000	39.7
Construction	431,093	153,900	35.7
Service	1,263,362	191,500	15.2
Fishing	36,263	4,600	12.7
Trade	991,490	47,900	4.8
Finance, insurance, and real estate	228,905	200	0.1
Industry not reported		9,900	
No returns		47,600	
Total of industries listed	5,189,546	1,446,900	27.9

Sources: Department of Labour, *Industrial and Geographic Distribution of Union Membership in Canada* (Ottawa, 1961); *Census of Canada, 1961,* vol. 3.2-1, table IA.

TABLE E13

Distribution of Male Labour Force by Occupational Group and Highest Level of Schooling, 1961

| Occupational Group | Highest Grade of School Attended Percentages | | | | | | |
	Elementary Only	Grades 9-11	Grades 12 and 13	Some University	University Degree	Total
Professional and technical	4.8	12.9	22.2	16.0	44.1	100.0
Managerial and proprietary	24.6	31.6	27.5	8.2	8.1	100.0
Clerical	19.8	39.1	32.0	7.2	1.9	100.0
Sales	21.8	40.2	27.6	7.2	3.2	100.0
Craftsmen and production process workers	52.7	33.8	11.5	1.6	0.4	100.0
Service and recreation	43.5	37.6	14.2	3.1	1.6	100.0
Transport and communication	51.7	36.5	9.8	1.7	0.3	100.0
Miners and related workers	61.3	28.8	7.3	2.2	0.4	100.0
Loggers and related workers	78.4	16.8	3.6	1.0	0.2	100.0
Fishermen, trappers and hunters	79.2	17.5	2.7	0.5	0.1	100.0
Labourers	66.9	24.3	6.4	2.2	0.2	100.0
Farmers and farm workers	68.2	24.3	5.8	1.3	0.4	100.0
Total	44.4	31.1	15.3	4.3	4.9	100.0

Source: *Census of Canada, 1961*, vol. 3.1-9, table 17.

TABLE E14

*Average Total Income[1] of Non-Farm Families
by the Occupational Group of the Head of the Family, 1961*

Occupational Group of Family Head	$	Rank
Professional and technical	8,850	1
Managerial and proprietary	8,671	2
Clerical	5,439	4
Sales	6,292	3
Craftsmen and production process workers	5,214	6
Service and recreation	4,998	8
Transport and communications	5,128	7
Miners and related workers	5,366	5
Loggers and related workers	3,693	10
Fishermen, trappers and hunters	3,044	12
Labourers	3,919	9
Farm workers[2]	3,375	11
Occupation not stated	4,980	–
All Occupations[2]	5,942	

[1]For year ending May 31, 1961.
[2]Farm operators are excluded.

Source: *Census of Canada, 1961*, vol. 4.1-4, table D8.

TABLE E15

Households and Their Contents, 1964

Contents	Number (000's)	Per cent of All Households
Hot air furnaces	2,658	55.9
Hot and cold water[1]	4,097	86.1
Baths and showers	4,021	84.5
Flush toilets		
one	3,743	78.7
two or more	516	10.9
Cook stoves[2]	3,170	66.6
Refrigerators[2]	4,520	95.0
Home freezers	970	20.4
Automatic washers[2]	985	20.7
Clothes dryers[2]	1,058	22.2
Automatic dishwashers[2]	104	2.2
Floor polishers	2,474	52.0
Window air conditioners	98	2.1
Cabinet record players	1,461	30.7
Telephones		
one	3,616	76.0
two or more	576	12.1
Radio		
one	2,705	56.9
two or more	1,860	39.1
T.V. sets	4,328	90.9
F.M. receivers	846	17.8
Power lawn mowers	1,731	36.4
Outboard motors	411	8.6
Automobiles		
one	2,947	61.9
two or more	571	12.0
Total Number of Households[3]	4,757	100.0

[1] Piped inside.
[2] Electric.
[3] A person or a group of persons occupying one dwelling.

Source: Dominion Bureau of Statistics, *Household Facilities and Equipment, 1964* (Ottawa, 1964).

TABLE E16

Income Classes, 1961

Income Class	Income Recipients[1]			Total Income		
	No. (000's)	Per cent	Accumulative Per cent	Million $	Per cent	Accumulative Per cent
Under $1,999	976	20.3	20.3	990	4.3	4.3
$ 2,000- 3,999	1,237	25.8	46.1	3,782	16.4	20.7
4,000- 5,999	1,302	27.2	73.3	6,413	27.7	48.4
6,000- 7,999	711	14.8	88.1	4,808	20.8	69.2
8,000- 9,999	313	6.5	94.6	2,801	12.1	81.3
10,000-14,999	188	3.9	98.5	2,313	10.0	91.3
15,000 and over	73	1.5	100.0	2,006	8.7	100.0
Totals	4,800	100.0		23,113	100.0	
Average Income		$4,815				
Median Income		$4,262				

[1] Non-farm families and unattached individuals.

Source: Dominion Bureau of Statistics, *Distribution of Non-Farm Income by Size, 1961* (Ottawa, 1964), tables 1 and 2.

TABLE E17

Corporations by Size of Assets, Equity, Sales, and Profits, 1962

Asset size group	Corporations		Assets	Equity	Sales	Profits
	Number	Per cent		Per cent		
Under $250,000	2,783	11.4	0.7	0.5	4.2	0.8
$ 250,000 to $ 499,999	9,336	38.0	5.1	4.2	8.9	3.9
500,000 to 999,999	5,699	23.3	6.2	5.1	10.0	4.8
1,000,000 to 4,999,999	5,097	20.8	16.6	15.4	21.0	13.9
5,000,000 to 9,999,999	726	3.0	7.9	8.1	8.4	7.5
10,000,000 to 24,999,999	485	2.0	11.7	12.0	11.4	11.5
25,000,000 to 49,999,999	176	0.7	9.6	10.3	7.3	10.1
50,000,000 to 99,999,999	122	0.5	13.1	13.9	10.6	15.3
100,000,000 and over	84	0.3	29.1	30.5	18.3	32.2
Total	24,508	100.0	100.0	100.0	100.0	100.0

Source: Dominion Bureau of Statistics, *Annual Report under the Corporations and Labour Unions Returns Act, 1962* (Ottawa, 1965), table IX.

F:

GOVERNMENT

TABLE F1

Federal Electorate, 1896-1965

		Potential Electorate		Voters	
	Estimated Adult Population[1] (000's)	Eligible Voters (000's)	Per Cent of Adult Population	Votes Polled (000's)	Per Cent of Eligible Voters
1896	2,801	1,358	48.5	899	66.2
1900	2,932	1,167	39.8	951	81.5
1904	3,269	1,385	42.4	1,031	74.4
1908	3,770	1,464	38.8	1,175	80.3
1911	4,145	1,821	43.9	1,308	71.8
1917	4,587	2,094	45.6	1,650	78.8
1921	4,966	4,435	89.3	3,119	70.3
1925	5,354	4,607	86.0	3,168	68.8
1926	5,434	4,665	85.8	3,273	70.2
1930	5,962	5,154	86.4	3,922	76.1
1935	6,551	5,918	90.3	4,453	75.2
1940	7,102	6,589	92.8	4,673	70.9
1945	7,533	6,952	92.3	5,305	76.3
1949	8,364	7,894	94.4	5,904	74.8
1953	9,085	8,402	92.5	5,702	67.9
1957	9,966	8,896	89.2	6,682	75.1
1958	10,214	9,131	89.4	7,357	80.6
1962	10,753	9,700	90.2	7,773	80.1
1963	10,896	9,911	91.0	7,959	80.3
1965	11,277	10,274	91.1	7,711	75.4

[1]Twenty years of age and over. Population totals taken from *Historical Statistics of Canada*, p. 14, and for years after 1961 from Dominion Bureau of Statistics Annual Intercensal Estimates. The proportion over 20 years was estimated from the nearest census.

Sources: Based on material from *Historical Statistics of Canada* (Toronto, 1965), p. 616, reprinted by permission of The Macmillan Company of Canada; Chief Electoral Officer, *Twenty-fifth General Election, 1962* (Ottawa, 1962); and *Twenty-sixth General Election, 1963* (Ottawa, 1963); and *Globe and Mail*, December 29, 1965.

TABLE F2

Seats and Votes by Party in Federal Elections, 1896-1965

	No. of Seats	Percent of Seats			Percent of Popular Vote		
		Liberal	Conservative	Other	Liberal	Conservative	Other
1896	213	54.9	41.8	3.3	45.1	46.3	8.6
1900	214	59.8	36.4	3.7	52.0	47.4	0.6
1904	214	64.9	35.0	0.0	52.5	46.9	0.6
1908	221	60.2	38.5	1.3	50.6	47.0	2.4
1911	221	38.9	60.2	.9	47.8	51.2	1.0
1917	235	34.9	65.1	0.0	41.9	58.1	0.0
1921	235	49.8	21.3	28.9	41.5	31.1	27.3
1925	245	41.2	47.3	11.4	39.9	46.3	13.6
1926	245	47.3	37.1	15.5	43.4	46.0	10.6
1930	245	35.9	55.9	8.2	43.9	49.0	7.0
1935	245	69.8	15.9	14.3	43.9	29.5	26.6
1940	245	72.6	15.9	11.4	54.9	30.7	14.4
1945	245	51.0	27.3	21.6	41.4	27.7	30.9
1949	262	72.5	15.6	11.8	50.1	29.8	20.1
1953	265	64.1	19.2	16.6	50.0	31.0	19.0
1957	265	39.6	42.3	18.1	42.3	39.0	18.6
1958	265	18.1	78.5	3.4	33.7	53.7	12.6
1962	265	37.7	43.8	18.5	37.2	37.3	25.5
1963	265	48.7	35.8	15.5	41.7	32.8	25.5
1965	265	49.4	36.6	13.9	40.2	32.4	27.4

Sources: Based on material from *Historical Statistics of Canada* (Toronto, 1965), p. 616, reprinted by permission of The Macmillan Company of Canada Limited; for 1962 and 1963, Peter Regenstreif, *The Diefenbaker Interlude* (Toronto, 1965), p. 31; for 1965, *The Globe and Mail*,

TABLE F3

Employment in the Federal Public Service, 1960

	Male	Female	Total	Per cent of all Federal Government Employees
Civilian				
Under Civil Service Act	95,372	36,575	131,947	28.3
Departmental Employees excluded from C.S. Act	14,618	5,100	19,718	4.2
Crown Corporations	135,600	14,796	150,396	32.3
Prevailing Rate Employees	18,464	5,327	23,791	5.1
Ships' Officers and Crews	—	—	3,033	0.7
Casual Employees	—	—	17,061	3.7
Total	264,054	61,798	345,946	74.2
Armed Forces	116,740	3,312	120,052	25.8
Total All Employees	380,794	65,110	465,998	100.0

All Government Employees as per cent of Total Labour Force = 7.3.

Source: *Royal Commission on Government Organization* (Ottawa, 1962), vol. 1, p. 309.

TABLE F4

Government Expenditure[1] by Major Function, 1933-1960

(millions of dollars)

	Social Welfare	Education	Health	Defence	Transportation and Communication	Veterans	All Other	Total
1933	133	107	35	15	89	51	520	950
1939	161	129	47	127	163	55	595	1,277
1943	125	151	52	4,016	293	65	870	5,572
1946	416	225	84	466	255	602	1,309	3,357
1951	662	498	256	1,417	544	209	1,773	5,359
1960	1,629	1,579	841	1,534	1,452	296	3,453	10,784

[1]Federal, provincial and municipal governments after elimination of inter-governmental transfers.

Source: Based on material from *Historical Statistics of Canada* (Toronto, 1965), p. 206, series G 83-95; reprinted by permission of The Macmillan Company of Canada Limited.

G:

EDUCATION

TABLE G1

Population in School by Province and Age, 1931, 1951, and 1961

Percentages

Provinces	10-14 years 1931	10-14 years 1951	10-14 years 1961	15-19 years 1931	15-19 years 1951	15-19 years 1961 Total	1961 Male	1961 Female
Newfoundland	—	94.6	96.4	—	38.4	51.7	54.3	49.1
Prince Edward Island	94.2	96.1	97.2	29.1	40.0	55.5	50.8	60.6
Nova Scotia	94.7	94.9	97.1	35.6	45.2	57.3	57.4	57.1
New Brunswick	90.9	94.0	97.0	31.4	40.6	56.7	56.5	57.0
Quebec	88.3	89.5	96.4	23.6	30.0	50.1	54.1	46.0
Ontario	96.3	94.0	97.5	38.6	43.7	62.9	65.8	60.0
Manitoba	94.9	95.0	97.6	36.0	44.0	62.1	64.5	57.5
Saskatchewan	95.9	96.2	96.9	35.0	49.8	65.5	65.4	65.7
Alberta	96.6	95.8	97.9	41.6	50.3	65.8	67.8	63.7
British Columbia	95.9	94.9	97.6	42.9	52.0	68.0	70.8	65.6

	10-14 years						15-19 years					
	1911	1921	1931	1941	1951	1961	1911	1921	1931	1941	1951	1961
Canada[1]	79.7	88.7	93.4	94.4	93.0	97.1	18.7	24.8	33.7	35.5	40.5	58.5

[1] Excluding Newfoundland to 1941 and Yukon and Northwest Territories to 1951.

Sources: *Census of Canada, 1931*, vol. IV, table 81; Dominion Bureau of Statistics, *Statistical Review of Canadian Education, 1951* (Ottawa, 1958), table 6; and *Census of Canada, 1961*, vol. 1.3-6, table 99.

TABLE G2

*Educational Level of Labour Force
by Sex, 1951 and 1961*

| | Percentages | | | |
| | 1951 | | 1961 | |
Educational Level	Male	Female	Male	Female
Elementary only	55.0	34.0	44.0	30.0
Some or completed High School	36.0	53.0	47.0	62.0
Some Post-High School	9.0	13.0	9.0	8.0
Total	100.0	100.0	100.0	100.0

Sources: Dominion Bureau of Statistics, *Statistical Review of Canadian Education, 1951* (Ottawa, 1958), table 33; and *Census of Canada, 1961*, vol. 3.1-13,

TABLE G3

*Undergraduate University Enrolment by Province,
1945-46 and 1964-65*

	Enrolment 1945-46	Enrolment 1964-65	Percentage Increase
Newfoundland	—	2,601	—
Prince Edward Island	179	802	348
Nova Scotia	2,139	8,109	279
New Brunswick	1,254	5,468	336
Quebec	13,075	54,759	318
Ontario	12,290	45,369	269
Manitoba	2,789	8,641	209
Saskatchewan	1,787	9,266	418
Alberta	1,478	11,929	707
British Columbia	3,095	17,497	465
Canada	38,086	164,441	331

Sources: Dominion Bureau of Statistics, *Survey of Higher Education 1963-64 and 1964-65* (Ottawa, 1966), table 1; and R. W. B. Jackson, "The Problem of Numbers in University Enrolment," (Mimeo) (Toronto, 1963), table XII.

TABLE G4

Full-Time University Enrolment and the College-Age Group,
1951-52.– 1962-63

	Full-Time Enrolment					
	Number (000's)			As Percentage of 18-24 Year Age Group		
	Male	Female	Total	Male	Female	Total
1951-52	50.2	13.3	63.5	6.7	1.7	4.2
1956-57	61.7	16.8	78.5	7.8	2.1	5.0
1960-61	86.2	27.7	113.9	10.2	3.3	6.7
1962-63	103.2	38.2	141.4	11.7	4.3	8.0

Source: Edward F. Sheffield, *Enrolment to 1976/77* (Canadian Universities Foundation, Ottawa, 1964), table 1.

TABLE G5

Degrees Granted by Canadian Universities and Colleges, 1921-1961

Selected Faculties

	Arts and Pure Science		Education		Law		Medicine	
	Total	Women	Total	Women	Total	Women	Total	Women
1921	1,414	521	1	–	398	14	404	14
1931	2,666	1,008	60	20	224	5	533	26
1941	3,664	1,141	149	37	260	4	562	25
1951	7,113	2,018	584	158	712	20	867	61
1961	9,228	2,836	2,430	903	697	35	842	65

Level of Degrees

	Bachelor[1]		Master		Doctorate	
	Total	Women	Total	Women	Total	Women
1921	3,627	664	218	48	24	1
1931	5,290	1,338	468	100	46	7
1941	6,576	1,582	673	71	75	5
1951	13,288	3,030	1,601	248	234	21
1961	20,240	5,211	2,447	466	305	26

[1] Including professional bachelor degrees and equivalent diplomas.

Sources: Higher Education Section, Education Division, Dominion Bureau of Statistics, Ottawa, and Ralph D. Mitchener, *First Degrees Awarded by Canadian Universities and Colleges Projected to 1976/77* (Ottawa, 1964).

TABLE G6

Occupations of the Fathers of University Students,[1] 1961-62

Occupation of father	Arts and Science	Education	Engineering	Law	Medicine	Dentistry	Pharmacy	Classical Colleges	Male labour force
				Percentages					
Owners and proprietors	13.7	9.0	10.1	14.9	12.3	21.3	12.9	16.6	9.9
Managers and superintendents	13.3	7.2	11.3	11.4	9.9	11.3	3.9	9.6	
Professional occupations	19.8	12.6	15.3	26.4	29.5	19.3	18.0	19.2	7.6
Engineers	2.5	1.4	4.5	4.0	2.6	1.5	1.1	2.5	0.9
Teaching professions	3.5	5.2	2.5	2.8	2.3	2.9	2.6	3.2	1.4
Physicians and surgeons	2.9	1.0	0.9	2.7	10.8	2.7	1.8	4.4	0.4
Dentists	0.3	0.1	0.6	0.9	1.1	4.3	0.7	0.7	0.1
Pharmacists	0.6	0.1	0.3	0.3	1.0	0.5	6.6	0.7	0.1
Legal professions	1.5	0.2	0.3	8.9	1.2	0.6	0.5	2.1	0.3
Other professions	8.5	4.7	6.2	6.8	10.5	6.8	4.7	5.6	4.4
Commercial and financial occupations	8.0	6.8	5.5	7.3	7.5	7.4	5.8	7.7	5.6
Clerical occupations	4.2	5.2	6.8	5.4	5.7	3.4	6.0	6.6	6.9
Manufacturing and mechanical occupations	10.4	10.4	14.3	10.3	9.5	13.0	14.3	10.4	22.0
Transportation and communication occupations	5.7	6.4	6.1	3.2	4.5	5.8	6.2	4.5	8.0
Construction occupations	3.9	6.6	5.3	2.4	3.7	3.4	5.2	5.3	6.3
Service and recreation occupations	6.2	5.3	4.5	5.4	2.3	3.4	7.0	4.2	8.5
Farmers	7.4	18.7	11.1	5.9	7.0	6.4	13.4	9.6	8.2
Other primary occupations	2.8	6.7	3.0	1.6	2.4	1.8	1.5	2.2	3.8
Farm and non-farm labourers	1.6	2.3	2.6	1.1	2.9	1.6	2.4	2.0	9.6
All other and not stated	3.0	2.8	4.1	4.7	2.8	1.9	3.4	2.1	3.6
Totals	100.0	100.0	100.0	100.0	100.0	100.0	100.0	100.0	100.0

[1] In Dentistry and Pharmacy percentages below 5 are questionable. In the other faculties the numbers are larger and the percentages more reliable.

Source: Dominion Bureau of Statistics, *University Student Expenditure and Income in Canada, 1961-62*, Part II (Ottawa, 1963), table 16.

TABLE G7

Male Wage Earners[1] by Educational Level and Amount of Earnings,[2] 1961

Earnings[2]	Elementary		Secondary		University[3]	
	No.	%	No.	%	No.	%
Less than $1,000	176,745	11.6	139,949	7.9	30,058	8.9
$1,000-1,999	232,322	15.3	144,151	8.2	21,963	6.5
$2,000-2,999	313,849	20.6	233,121	13.2	18,236	5.4
$3,000-3,999	389,565	25.6	379,240	21.5	32,202	9.7
$4,000-4,999	250,540	16.4	386,816	21.9	40,792	12.1
$5,000-5,999	102,130	6.7	238,913	13.6	43,039	12.8
$6,000-6,999	34,291	2.2	116,524	6.6	39,469	11.7
$7,000-9,999	19,568	1.3	92,869	5.3	68,514	20.4
$10,000 and over	4,098	0.3	31,326	1.8	41,743	12.4
Total	1,523,108	100.0	1,762,909	100.0	336,016	100.0
Average Earnings	$ 2,964		$ 3,911		$ 5,699	

[1]Includes only those wage earners, 15 years of age and over, who reported earnings.
[2]This refers to the total amount of money received by wage earners as cash wages or salary, before deductions such as income tax, union dues, etc. Such forms of remuneration as free board and payment in kind are not included.
[3]Includes also those who have had only some university education.

Source: *Census of Canada, 1961*, vol. 3.3-5, table 17.

TABLE G8

Minimum Years of Educational Attainment of Male Labour Force,
Aged 25-34 and 55-64, Canada 1961 and United States 1960

Minimum Attainment	Age Group	Per Cent of Male Labour Force		Percentage by which U.S. exceeds Canada
		Canada	United States	
8 years elementary school	25-34	81.5	88.9	9
	55-64	55.5	68.8	24
4 years high school	25-34	28.2	57.2	103
	55-64	16.9	26.1	54
University degree	25-34	6.0	14.7	145
	55-64	4.2	7.0	67

Source: Economic Council of Canada, *Second Annual Review* (Ottawa, 1965), table 4-5.

H:

LEISURE

TABLE H1
Amusement and Recreation Establishments,
1931, 1951, and 1961

	1931 No.	1951 No.	1961 No.
Regular theatres	984	1,799	959
Halls for motion picture exhibition	*	612	253
Outdoor motion picture theatres	*	82	148
Legitimate theatres, music halls	20	22	8
Theatrical producers, road companies	*	31	7
Bands and orchestras	*	12	52
Billiard parlours	⎫	1,341	1,315
Bowling alleys	⎬ 1,537	428	829
Bowling and billiards	⎭		
Dancehalls, studios and schools	146	387	250
Athletic arenas, grounds, etc.	14	47	65
Bicycle rentals	*	49	4
Boat and canoe rentals	117	148	149
Golf courses	108	37	195
Race tracks	*	1	25
Riding academies	11	42	120
Amusement parks	36	22	28
Amusement concessions	34	42	46
Coin-operated amusement	10	77	41
Others	283	239	659
Total amusement and recreation establishments	3,300	5,564	5,280
Total amusement receipts ($000's)	53,231	150,973	252,864
Total receipts all service trades ($000's)	249,456	1,085,757	2,995,760
Amusement receipts as percentage of all service receipts	21.3	13.9	8.4

*Not available.

Sources: *Census of Canada, 1931*, vol. XI, table 1A; *Census of Canada, 1951*, vol. VIII, table 21; *Census of Canada, 1961*, vol. 6.2-11, table 42.

TABLE H2

Contribution of Beer, Wine and Spirits to the Apparent Total Consumption of Absolute Alcohol, 1961

	Beer	Wine	Spirits	Gallons per Capita[1]
Newfoundland	63.0	5.5	31.5	0.92
Prince Edward Island	—	—	—	—
Nova Scotia	50.5	10.5	39.0	1.14
New Brunswick	49.5	12.0	38.5	1.03
Quebec	68.0	7.0	25.0	1.53
Ontario	61.0	7.0	32.0	1.79
Manitoba	64.0	6.0	30.0	1.56
Saskatchewan	61.0	8.0	31.0	1.35
Alberta	61.0	6.0	33.0	1.59
British Columbia	54.0	7.0	39.0	1.66
Canada	62.0	7.0	31.0	1.59
Selected Other Countries				
United States 1959	48.5	11.0	40.5	1.61
France 1955	12.5	75.5	12.0	5.87
Italy 1957	1.5	91.0	7.5	3.25
United Kingdom 1958	81.0	4.0	15.0	1.25
Sweden 1958	24.0	11.0	65.0	1.07

[1]Imperial gallons per capita 15 years and older.

Source: Alcoholism and Drug Addiction Research Foundation, *Twelfth Annual Report 1962* (Toronto), appendix III, table II.

TABLE H3

Number of Titles and Circulation of
Daily and Weekly Newspapers, 1921-1959

	Number of Titles		Circulation (000's)	
	Dailies	Weeklies	Dailies	Weeklies
1921	111	870	1,716	2,471
1931	111	893	2,233	3,547
1941	90	757	2,250	2,328
1951	95	857	3,556	3,977
1961	110	897	4,064	2,806
1963	109	855	4,213	*

*Not available.

Sources: *Royal Commission on Publications, Report* (Ottawa, 1961), appendix K, table 16; Dominion Bureau of Statistics, *Canada Year Book, 1962* (Ottawa, 1962), p. 864, and *Canada Year Book, 1965* (Ottawa, 1965), p. 848.

TABLE H4
Public Libraries by Province, 1962

	Number of Libraries	Population Served	Stocks of Books, Periodicals, etc.	Circulation
Newfoundland	3	470,000	315,082	704,410
Prince Edward Island	2	106,000	112,709	238,762
Nova Scotia	13	486,381	424,956	2,074,138
New Brunswick	7	241,448	205,865	952,359
Quebec	222	2,934,704	2,430,228	4,712,062
Ontario	315	5,961,679	7,636,775	35,718,670
Manitoba	18	514,903	501,818	2,833,385
Saskatchewan	59	430,144	689,032	2,407,122
Alberta	144	857,209	1,286,105	5,394,473
British Columbia	77	1,392,184	1,938,152	10,033,812
Yukon and Northwest Territories	14	12,423	29,637	11,380
Total	874	13,407,075	15,570,359	65,080,573

Source: Dominion Bureau of Statistics, *Preliminary Statistics of Education, 1963-64* (Ottawa, 1964), table 32.

TABLE H5

Part-Time Adult Education, 1962-63

Courses[1]		Enrolments
Diploma and Degree		201,686
Elementary Level	6,769	
Secondary Level	107,338	
University Level	87,579	
Professional and Vocational		582,673
Total Diploma, Degree and Professional		784,359
Social Education		201,922
Cultural		90,904
Total All Enrolments		1,077,185
Total Attendance at public lectures and film showings, etc.		3,972,002

[1]Including correspondence courses.

Source: Dominion Bureau of Statistics, *Survey of Adult Education, 1962-63* (Ottawa, 1965), table 1.

TABLE H6

Scientific Books (Including Re-editions)
Published in Selected Countries, 1960[1]

Category of Book	Canada	USA[2]	UK[3]	USSR	Sweden
Pure Science	175	1,089	1,879	5,061	538
Applied Science	535	1,876	3,882	36,931	1,042
Social Science	674	1,496	3,400	14,403	476
Geography & History	296	2,210	2,545	2,261	715
Philology	89	228	734	2,026	426
Philosophy	35	480	457	612	45
Total Above	1,804	7,379	12,897	61,294	3,242
Total All Books	2,743	15,012	23,783	76,064	5,825

[1]The data show the number of books published by subject, each title being counted as one unit. They are understood, unless otherwise stated, to cover all non-periodical publications, including pamphlets, first editions of originals and (new) translations or re-editions, and the more important government reports.
[2]Books only, excluding pamphlets, which are defined as works of less than 49 pages. The statistics refer only to the production of the book trade and omit a large part of total book production (e.g. publications of federal, state and local government, universities, churches, etc.).
[3]Including books published in Ireland. Books and pamphlets priced at less than sixpence are omitted.

Source: United Nations, *Statistical Year Book 1961* (New York, 1961), table 179, pp. 630-633. Copyright United Nations, 1967. Reproduced by permission.

I:

DEVIANT
BEHAVIOUR

TABLE II

Summary Convictions[1] and Sentences, 1961

Offence	Suspended	Suspended with Probation	Sentence Fine	Jail	Other	Total
Prohibited parking	5,229	111	1,817,025	40	–	1,822,405
Highway traffic	8,198	231	661,653	303	–	670,385
City traffic	2,085	103	201,486	50	–	203,724
Drunkenness	10,861	352	86,753	8,826	–	106,792
Other liquor	713	481	64,586	963	–	66,743
All others	14,469	4,848	194,015	17,575	8,327	239,234
Total	41,555	6,126	3,025,518	27,757	8,327	3,109,283

[1]The less serious offences tried by magistrates and justices of the peace.

Source: Dominion Bureau of Statistics, *Statistics of Criminal and Other Offences, 1961* (Ottawa, 1963), table 15.

TABLE 12

Indictable Offences[1] and Sentences, 1961

Offence	Suspended	Suspended with Probation	Sentence				Total
			Fine	Jail or Penitentiary	Death		
Against the person	565	463	2,330	2,236	12		5,606
Against property with violence	764	1,500	183	5,416	–		7,863
without violence	2,710	4,035	4,412	8,685	–		19,842
Forgery	120	173	27	976	–		1,296
Others	323	370	1,556	1,823	–		4,072
Total	4,482	6,541	8,508	19,136	12		38,679

[1]By number of persons convicted. The indictable offences are the more serious ones tried by superior courts after committal by magistrates.

Source: Dominion Bureau of Statistics, *Statistics of Criminal and Other Offences, 1961* (Ottawa, 1963), table 8.

TABLE 13

Convictions of Indictable Offences by Age, Sex and Urban-Rural Residence, 1961

Age		Urban Number	Rate[1]	Rural Number	Rate[1]	Not Stated Number	Total Number	Rate[1]
16-19 years[2]	Male	8,262	23.1	2,078	10.0	239	10,579	18.7
	Female	497	1.3	92	0.5	10	599	1.1
20-24 years	Male	6,093	14.8	1,524	8.6	229	7,846	13.4
	Female	569	1.3	57	0.4	9	635	1.1
25-34 years	Male	6,524	7.0	1,291	3.9	222	8,037	6.4
	Female	695	0.8	82	0.3	10	787	0.6
35 years and over	Male	6,143	2.6	1,059	1.0	263	7,465	2.1
	Female	871	0.3	105	0.1	8	984	0.3
Not stated	Male	670	–	265	–	654	1,589	–
	Female	114	–	10	–	34	158	–
Total	Male	27,692	6.7	6,217	3.5	1,607	35,516	6.0
	Female	2,746	0.6	346	0.2	71	3,163	0.5

[1]Per 1,000 population of age and area group. Rates shown are slightly lower than they actually are because of the "not stated" categories.

[2]Population of Canada 16-19 years calculated by interpolating from single years of age according to urban/rural ratio for age group, 15-19 years.

Sources: Dominion Bureau of Statistics, *Statistics of Criminal and Other Offences, 1961* (Ottawa, 1963), table 4; and *Census of Canada, 1961*, vol. 1.2-2, table 21.

TABLE I4

Convictions of Indictable Offences by Place of Birth, 1961

Place of Birth	Number of Convictions	Total Population	Rate[1]
Canada	33,543	15,394,000	2.18
United Kingdom	863	970,000	0.89
Other Commonwealth	51	48,000	1.06
Europe	2,074	1,468,000	1.41
Asia	68	58,000	1.17
United States	297	284,000	1.05
Other	31	17,000	1.82
Not Stated	1,752		
Total	38,679	18,239,000	2.12

[1]Per 1,000 population.

Sources: Dominion Bureau of Statistics, *Statistics of Criminal and Other Offences, 1961* (Ottawa, 1963), p. 19; and *Census of Canada, 1961*, vol. 1.2-7, table 48.

TABLE 15

Juvenile Delinquents by Offence and Sentence, 1961

Offence		
Type	Number	Percentage
Theft and having in possession	6,076	40.0
Breaking and entering	3,415	22.4
Other property offences	1,174	7.7
Incorrigibility	842	5.5
Immorality	238	1.5
Common assault	223	1.5
Robbery and extortion	96	0.6
Arson	74	0.5
Indecent assault	70	0.5
Various other delinquencies	3,007	19.8
Total	15,215	100.0

Sentence			
Type	Number		Percentage
Probation		7,985	52.4
Supervision of courts	7,341		48.2
Care of parents	644		4.2
Fine or restitution		2,148	14.1
Training school		1,974	13.0
Reprimand		544	3.6
Indefinite detention		89	0.6
Mental hospital		9	0.1
Final disposition suspended		2,466	16.2
Total		15,215	100.0

Source: Dominion Bureau of Statistics, *Juvenile Delinquents, 1961* (Ottawa, 1963), pp. 12 and 14.

TABLE 16

Juvenile Delinquents by Parents' Birthplace, 1961

	One Parent Born in Canada		Both Parents Born Outside	
Place of Birth	Father	Mother	Father	Mother
Canada	565	706	–	–
United Kingdom	303	362	344	367
Other Commonwealth	13	5	18	18
Europe	197	83	898	874
Asia	11	4	19	20
United States	89	88	44	48
Other	3	1	6	6
Not Stated	90	22	1,416	1,412
Total	1,271	1,271	2,745	2,745

Total with one or both parents born outside Canada   4,016
Total with both parents born in Canada   11,199
                                                        Total 15,215

Source: Dominion Bureau of Statistics, *Juvenile Delinquents, 1961* (Ottawa, 1963), table 11.

TABLE 17

Juvenile Delinquents by School Grade, Age and Sex, 1961
(Continued on next page)

Age	\multicolumn{11}{c}{Males — Grade}

Age	1-4	5	6	7	8	9	10	11+ Grades	Auxiliary Grades	Not Stated	Total
7	28	–	–	–	–	–	–	–	1	1	30
8	117	–	–	–	–	–	–	–	–	4	121
9	261	21	3	–	–	–	–	–	2	7	294
10	297	121	36	2	–	–	–	–	5	14	475
11	258	236	210	38	7	–	–	–	4	18	771
12	207	336	478	359	53	4	1	–	11	30	1,479
13	116	281	507	700	477	68	8	–	24	73	2,254
14	94	208	434	908	1,044	661	77	7	54	128	3,615
15	88	188	328	773	996	1,201	506	71	64	221	4,436
Not Stated	–	–	–	–	1	–	–	–	1	27	29
Total	1,466	1,391	1,996	2,780	2,578	1,934	592	78	166	523	13,504

Juvenile Delinquents by School Grade, Age and Sex, 1961
(Continued from preceding page)

Females

Age	1-4	5	6	7	8	9	10	11+ Grades	Auxiliary Grades	Not Stated	Total
7	1	–	–	–	–	–	–	–	–	–	1
8	6	–	–	–	–	–	–	–	–	–	6
9	8	1	–	–	–	–	–	–	–	1	10
10	14	13	3	–	–	–	–	–	–	1	31
11	13	11	17	4	–	–	–	–	1	–	46
12	10	16	28	41	10	–	–	–	3	3	111
13	9	21	44	81	65	19	–	–	2	11	252
14	12	21	52	145	164	134	19	–	11	19	577
15	12	26	44	94	161	209	78	4	7	41	676
Not Stated	–	–	–	–	–	–	–	–	–	1	1
Total	85	109	188	365	400	362	97	4	24	77	1,711

Source: Dominion Bureau of Statistics, *Juvenile Delinquents, 1961* (Ottawa, 1963), table 14.

TABLE 18

Urban[1] Police Departments by Size of City, 1961

City Population	Total Population	Personnel Police	Personnel Civilian	Personnel per 1,000 Population
Over 100,000	4,992,332	8,865	1,353	2.0
50,000-100,000	1,390,614	2,015	175	1.6
25,000- 50,000	1,633,525	1,833	129	1.2
10,000- 25,000	1,597,089	1,748	159	1.2
Under 10,000	1,868,321	2,121	178	1.2
Total	11,481,881	16,582	1,994	1.6

[1]Communities of 750 and over.

Source: Dominion Bureau of Statistics, *Police Administration Statistics, 1961* (Ottawa, 1962), table 6.

TABLE 19

Patients in Mental Hospitals, 1932-1961

	Number	Rate[1]
1932	33,290	317
1941	45,135	392
1951	55,395	395
1961	66,546	365

[1]Per 100,000 population.

Source: Dominion Bureau of Statistics, *Mental Health Statistics, 1962* (Ottawa, 1964), vol. 1, table 4.

TABLE I10

First Admissions to Mental Hospitals by Sex, 1932-1962

	Male		Female		Total	
	Number	Rate[1]	Number	Rate[1]	Number	Rate[1]
1932	3,340	66	2,434	51	5,774	55
1941	3,942	67	3,122	56	7,064	61
1951	5,911	84	4,981	72	10,892	78
1961	14,300	155	13,521	150	27,821	153
1962	15,394	164	14,511	158	29,905	161

[1]Per 100,000 population.

Source: Dominion Bureau of Statistics, *Mental Health Statistics, 1962* (Ottawa, 1964), vol. 1, table 12.

TABLE I11

Deaths Attributed to Alcoholism and Cirrhosis of the Liver, 1901-1961

	Death Rates		Cirrhosis Deaths Per 1,000 Deaths From All Causes
	From Alcoholism[1]	From Cirrhosis[1]	From All Causes[2]	
1901	2.1	8.8	1,751	2.7
1911	5.8	9.0	1,467	3.5
1921	2.3	5.9	1,153	2.9
1931	2.4	6.1	1,009	3.5
1941	1.2	6.6	998	4.1
1951	[3]	7.0	897	4.8
1956	[3]	8.8	828	6.4
1961	[3]	9.8	770	7.3

[1]Rates per 100,000 population, aged 20 and over.
[2]Rate per 100,000 population, all ages.
[3]Not reported after 1949.

Sources: Robert E. Popham and Wolfgang Schmidt, *Statistics of Alcohol Use and Alcoholism in Canada, 1871-1956* (Toronto, 1958), table IV-3; Alcoholism and Drug Addiction Research Foundation, *Thirteenth Annual Report, 1963* (Toronto), table VIII, reprinted by permission of the University of Toronto Press.

TABLE I12

Narcotic Addiction, 1962[1]

	Criminal Addicts[2]	Medical Addicts[3]	Professional Addicts[4]	Total	Percentage by Region
British Columbia	1,888	35	5	1,928	53.9
Ontario	834	104	57	995	27.8
Quebec	198	91	42	331	9.3
Prairies	210	36	20	266	7.4
Atlantic Provinces	6	40	10	56	1.6
Canada	3,136	306	134	3,576	100.0

[1]As officially recorded by the Department of National Health anJ Welfare.
[2]Convicted under the Narcotic Control Act and/or having a "criminal background" or "criminal associations".
[3]As a result of medical treatment.
[4]Members of health professions with access to narcotics.

Source: Alcoholism and Drug Addiction Research Foundation, *Thirteenth Annual Report, 1963* (Toronto), table IX; reprinted by permission of the University of Toronto Press.

Deviant Behaviour by Province, 1961

	Indictable Offenders[1]	Rank of Province	Juvenile Delinquents[2]	Rank of Province	Divorces[3]	Rank of Province	Illegitimate Births[4]	Rank of Province	Suicides[5]	Rank of Province	Alcoholics[6]	Rank of Province
Alberta	476	1	500	3	78.0	2	6.2	4	8.9	3	1,550	6
British Columbia	464	2	684	1	85.8	1	6.9	1	11.8	1	2,380	2
Manitoba	391	3	435	4	33.9	4	6.3	3	7.6	5	1,970	4
Ontario	337	4	628	2	43.9	3	3.5	10	8.8	4	2,440	1
Nova Scotia	296	5	382	5	33.2	5	6.9	1	5.2	7	1,460	7
Saskatchewan	293	6	150	10	27.1	7	5.9	5	10.2	2	1,170	9
Newfoundland	273	7	374	7	1.3	10	4.3	8	3.7	10	915	10
Quebec	244	8	270	8	6.6	9	3.6	9	4.6	9	2,340	3
New Brunswick	191	9	379	6	32.4	6	4.4	7	5.0	8	1,230	8
Prince Edward Island	64	10	243	9	7.6	8	4.8	6	6.7	6	1,640	5
Canada	328		449		36.0		4.5		7.5		2,140	

[1] Rate per 100,000 population, 16 years and older.
[2] Rate per 100,000 population, 7-15 years of age.
[3] Rate per 100,000 population.
[4] Per cent of live births.
[5] Rate per 100,000 population.
[6] Estimated alcoholics per 100,000 population, aged 20 and over.

Source: P. J. Giffen, "Rates of Crime and Delinquency," table 18, from W. T. McGrath (ed.) *Crime and Its Treatment in Canada* (Toronto, 1965), p. 88; reprinted by permission of the author and The Macmillan Company of Canada Limited.

J:

ILLNESS
AND MORTALITY

TABLE J1

*Per Capita Expenditures on Personal Health Services
by Type of Expenditure and Percentage of
Gross National Expenditure, 1931-61*

Type of Expenditure	Cost in $			
	1931	1941	1951	1961
Physicians' services	6.13	5.80	10.92	21.01
Dentists' services	1.84	1.90	3.64	6.51
Hospital services	5.59	7.75	23.30	50.65
Other health services	2.51	2.09	2.96	6.31
Administrative cost of health insurance	.28	.43	1.79	3.93
All services[1]	16.35	17.96	42.62	88.41
Prescribed drugs	*	*	3.06	6.11
Total expenditure	16.35	17.96	45.68	94.52
Total expenditure as a percentage of per capita Gross National Expenditure	3.61	2.48	3.02	4.61

[1]Columns may not add up due to rounding.
*Not available.

Source: *Royal Commission on Health Services* (Ottawa, 1964), vol. 1, table 11-2.

TABLE J2

Hospital Admissions[1] and Days of Care, 1948-1960

	1948	1950	1958	1960
Admissions[2]	111	119	142	145
Average length of stay in days	10.0	9.9	9.8	9.9
Days of care[2]	1,318	1,411	1,578	1,656

[1]Does not include federal hospitals or new-born admissions.
[2]Per 1,000 population.

Source: *Royal Commission on Health Services* (Ottawa, 1964), vol. 1, table 8-4.

TABLE J3

*Inhabitants per Hospital Bed and per Physician
for Selected Countries, 1957-1959[1]*

	Inhabitants per Hospital Bed	Inhabitants per Physician
Canada	90	910
U.S.A.[2]	110	800
England and Wales	110	960[4]
Scotland	90	780[4]
Sweden	80	1,100
New Zealand	90	700[5]
Chile	260[3]	1,700[4]
Japan	120	940

[1]Ratio averaged over three years.
[2]Includes Alaska and Hawaii for 1959.
[3]Data refer to government establishments only and are average of 2 years only.
[4]Only 1 year available.
[5]Average of 2 years only.

Source: United Nations, *Compendium of Social Statistics, 1963* (New York, 1963), p. 155, table 17. Copyright, United Nations, 1967. Reproduced by permission.

TABLE J4

Infant Mortality Rates,[1] 1921-1963

	Neo-natal[2]	Post-neo-natal[3]	Total Infant Mortality[4]
Average 1921-25	43	41	84
Average 1931-35	38	38	76
1941	31	30	61
1951	22.6	15.9	38.5
1961	18.0	9.2	27.2
1963	18.1	8.2	26.3

[1]Per 1,000 live births.
[2]Under 28 days.
[3]4 weeks to 1 year.
[4]Under 1 year.
Source: Dominion Bureau of Statistics, *Vital Statistics, 1963* (Ottawa, 1965), tables D12, D16 and D18.

TABLE J5

Crude Death Rates[1] from Selected Causes, 1926-1963

	Average 1926-30	Average 1931-35	Average 1936-40	Average 1941-45	Average 1946-50	Average 1951-55	Average 1956-60	Year 1963	% Change 1926-30 to 1963
Cardiovascular-renal disease[2]	278.1	281.6	314.4	391.5	406.3	414.0	399.9	390.2	+40.3
Cancer[3]	88.0	100.9	113.8	123.3	129.3	128.7	128.6	132.7	+50.8
Accidents	58.7	52.3	55.8	60.5	58.8	57.4	55.1	54.3	− 7.5
Tuberculosis	80.3	65.5	56.3	50.0	37.0	14.6	6.2	4.0	−95.0
Influenza, bronchitis, pneumonia	134.0	100.6	97.4	69.0	55.2	45.9	44.9	44.4	−66.9
Four communicable diseases[4]	29.1	14.7	13.4	8.7	4.5	2.4	1.1	0.6	−97.9

[1]Per 100,000 population.
[2]Includes diseases of heart (including rheumatic fever) and arteries, intracranial lesions, chronic nephritis.
[3]Includes Hodgkin's disease, leukemia and aleukemia.
[4]Includes diphtheria, whooping cough, measles, and scarlet fever.

Source: Dominion Bureau of Statistics, *Vital Statistics, 1963* (Ottawa, 1965), table G.

LIST OF TABLES

DEMOGRAPHIC STRUCTURE (*p. 41*)

MARRIAGE AND FAMILY (*p. 57*)

GOVERNMENT (*p. 105*)

EDUCATION (*p. 111*)

ILLNESS AND MORTALITY (*p. 145*)

THE EDITOR

John Porter was born in Vancouver. He is a graduate of the London School of Economics and Political Science, University of London, England. He joined the faculty of Carleton University in 1949, where he has been successively lecturer, assistant professor and associate professor. In 1963 he was appointed Professor of Sociology and Director of the Social Sciences Division of Carleton University. He held the latter position until the end of the 1965-66 academic year. He has published various papers on social class and elites in Canada and on other aspects of Canadian society. He is co-editor of *Canadian Society: Sociological Perspectives*. He is the author of *The Vertical Mosaic: An Analysis of Social Class and Power in Canada* which was published in 1965. For this book he received the MacIver Award of the American Sociological Association. In 1966 he was awarded the D.Sc. (Econ.) degree from the University of London for his work in sociology.

THE CARLETON LIBRARY